KU-197-661

PŁ 2-25p

THE
ASTROLOGY
YEARBOOK

Dedication
To my husband Denys, whose Taurean patience,
warmth and gentle humour mean so much to me

The Author
Joan Moore is a journalist and an author who has studied and written
extensively on astrological, metaphysical and occult subjects. An
acknowledged authority worldwide on matters feline, Joan has a
particular interest in the esoteric aspect and has written a thesis on
the myth and legend of the cat throughout the ages. She is a Fellow
of the Zoological Society of London and Editor of the UK's
foremost publications on cats: *Cat World* and *Show Cats* magazines
and the *Cat World Annual*.

CLB 3328
© 1994 CLB Publishing
This edition published 1995 by Parragon Book Service Ltd
Unit 13-17 Avonbridge Trading Estate, Atlantic Road
Avonmouth, Bristol BS11 9QD
All rights reserved
ISBN 1-7525-1099-1
Printed in Italy

Colour artwork
© Nadine Wickenden

Photographs
The publisher wishes to thank the following
photographers and picture agencies who have
supplied the photographs that are reproduced in
this book, and whose copyright images they are:
Frank Lane Picture Agency; John Glover; Images
Colour Library and Horizon.

Editor
Philip de Ste. Croix

Designer
Jill Coote

Production
Ruth Arthur
Sally Connolly
Neil Randles
Karen Staff

Director of production
Gerald Hughes

Typesetting
SX Composing Ltd, Essex

Colour reproduction:
Scantrans PTE Ltd, Singapore

Printed and bound in Italy

THE ASTROLOGY YEARBOOK

JOAN MOORE

||| •PARRALLEL• |||

Introduction

The ancients perceived the World as a living being, and Man as the World in miniature. It was held that the movements of both World and Man corresponded, and given that the former could be ascertained, the destiny of the latter could be calculated. Thus astrology evolved – to interpret the events and nature of Man's life by the movements of the planets and stars. Astrology has guided mankind from approximately the third millennium BC and was recognised as a science until the 18th century AD. Thereafter, following long associations with witchcraft and opposed by religion and new philosophies, astrology fell out of general favour.

The Astrology Yearbook contains a wealth of fascinating astrological lore. This collective knowledge, together with the myth and legend surrounding the mysteries of the Zodiac, offers enlightenment and insight into an absorbing subject. Explanatory text and diagrams at the end of the book will further clarify the meaning of the astrological terms which are used throughout.

Of all the planets, do you know which one rules your Sun sign? Did you know that your own ruling planet has its own personality? Which flowers, trees and gemstones hold a special significance for you? Are you in the most appropriate profession? Find out from the listed birth dates of famous people, past and present, who shares *your* birthday. Why are you drawn to a particular person, place or pastime? *The Astrology Yearbook* reveals the answers, helping you to develop a new understanding of yourself and your relationships with others.

Because of their representation of divine and creative mysteries, certain numbers and their combinations are said to hold magical powers. A glimpse at the ancient art of numerology, with its origins in the occult philosophy of the Hebraic Kabal and beyond, can also be found in this book. Quickly learn how to calculate the numbers which are lucky for you – and discover the mystical significance of those numbers. Discover how a change of name could mean a change of character or destiny – did you know that the ancients believed a name change could make strong a person in failing health? This belief perhaps explains why in the Old Testament of the Bible, God said to Abram: 'Thy name shall be Abraham . . .'

When you are in a position to put your newly acquired knowledge to positive use, why not complement your 'spirituality' by using, on a day to day basis, the symbols designated to your Sun sign? Wear your special gemstone and colours and encourage the benign forces of the planets those symbols represent. Select your symbols instinctively, intuitively each day and discover a significant improvement in your wellbeing.

Exquisitely illustrated and sensitively written, this book provides a delightful way to record birthdays, anniversaries and special days to remember. Enlightening and enriching realisation of your inner self, it may also reveal much that has previously remained secret and hidden! The message of *The Astrology Yearbook* is 'Know thyself' – this is the key which can unlock the door to a more spiritually fulfilled and rewarding future.

Astrology is defined as 'the art of divining the fate or destiny of persons from the juxtaposition of the Sun, Moon and planets'. It can also be said that what Man *does* is influenced by the planets and *how he does it* is influenced by his Zodiacal sign.

Devised by the Babylonians around 500 BC, the Zodiac is an intellectual concept. It is envisaged as a band of sky extending 8° either side of the ecliptic, the circle on the celestial sphere (an imaginary sphere surrounding the Earth on which astronomers locate celestial objects) which represents the path of the Sun's annual journey through the fixed constellations as we see it from Earth. The Zodiac comprises twelve equal sections, each representing one of the twelve Zodiacal signs, and each named after the constellation which once was found in it.

The Zodiacal circle, with each progressing month, symbolises the evolution of what I describe as the 'archetypal individual' – perceived by Swiss psychologist Carl Jung and others as an imaginary perfect, typical being having human form. The Zodiacal year begins with Aries, progressing through Taurus, Gemini, Cancer, Leo, Virgo, Libra, Scorpio, Sagittarius, Capricorn, Aquarius and finally to the twelfth Sun sign, Pisces.

The first six Sun signs of the Zodiac, Aries through to Virgo, relate to the formation of the individual, from the primitive self-drive of Aries to industrious Virgo, recognising and adapting to the social sphere. The final six Sun signs begin with Libra, which desires harmonious relationships on a one-to-one basis. The gradual integration of self into society is revealed until, with Aquarius, the need to be an integral *part* of society is established. Pisces, however, requires something more than mere socialisation. To achieve fulfilment, Pisces

CAPRICORN • SAGITTARIUS • SCORPIO • LIBRA • VIRGO • LEO • CANCER • GEMINI • TAURUS • ARIES • PISCES • AQUARIUS

0°

Earth
Fire
Air
Water
Masculine
Feminine
Cardinal
Fixed
Mutable

seeks to attain a mystical 'oneness' and a sense of harmony with the Universe.

The ancients were divided in their perception of Pisces. Some felt that this was the first Zodiacal sign, symbolising the emergence of spirit from the primordial deep, seeking enlightenment and self-knowledge. Others designated Pisces as the last stage in the development of the archetypal individual and this thinking prevails today. Thus, the progression of the Zodiac advances from the drive of 'self' through the socialisation of 'self' to the discovery of 'inner self'.

First or last, the ongoing cycle of life, represented by the Zodiacal wheel, has no beginning or end – simply eternal continuity. As Manilius, a Latin poet of the first century AD, writes in his astrological epic *Astronomica*: 'Being born, we begin to die; and the end depends upon the beginning'.

With the assistance of Egyptian astrologers, the Julian calendar was devised and introduced by Julius Caesar in 46 BC. This system fixed the year at 365.25 days with an extra day added to the calendar every fourth and centenary year to accommodate the extra quarter-days. The Gregorian calendar, which only recognises a century year as a leap year if it is divisible by 400, was introduced into Catholic countries in 1582 by Pope Gregory XIII. Generally accepted in the rest of Christian Europe in 1752, this version is still used today.

For the purpose of the diary-date format of *The Astrology Yearbook*, the Gregorian calendar, beginning with January and ending with December, has been used. Astrological information, however, has been arranged in accordance with the Zodiacal year, beginning at 0° in Aries and ending with twelfth Sun sign, Pisces.

J.M.

January

1	
2	
3	
4	
5	
6	
7	

Standing at the Gate of the New Year is the Roman god Janus, protector of gateways and passageways, who kept the gate of heaven. Double-headed Janus, looking back at what has been and forward to what will be, was also known as the Lord of Beginnings, and it is from his name that the word January derives.

'Take from my mouth the wish of happy years'
William Shakespeare, Richard II, Act i, Sc. 3

*'And other Spirits there are standing apart
Upon the Forehead of the Age to come'*
John Keats, Poems – 1817

January

Astrologically, Saturn, the ruling planet of Capricorn (22nd December – 20th January) symbolises limitation, responsibilities, control and discipline. Conversely, Saturn typifies wisdom, worth, stability, security and brings success through diligence and perseverance. Saturn is also the ancient ruler of Aquarius – to which modern astrologers have since designated the planet Uranus.

'. . . You'd be so lean, that blasts of January
Would blow you through and through. Now, my fair'st friend,
I would I had some flowers o' the spring that might
Become your time of day . . .'
William Shakespeare, The Winter's Tale, *Act iv, Sc. 4*

14th January 1559 marked the coronation of Elizabeth I of England. Dr John Dee, Elizabeth's personal astrologer, predicted that this date would be the most propitious for the ceremony. His prediction proved to be correct – the reign of Queen Elizabeth I was known as the 'Golden Age'.

8

9

10

11

12

13

14

January

15

16

17

18

19

20

In Babylonian myth, Capricorn is seen as the Fish-tailed god Ea – sometimes known as the Antelope of the Sea – emerging from the deep to teach wisdom to Man. There is also a traditional association with Aquarius, the Water Carrier or the God with Two Streams. These were seen by some astrologers to be divine wisdom bestowed upon mankind. For the Egyptians they were life-giving forces imparted by the Nile god Hapi.

Aquarius

21st January – 18th February

A Masculine • Positive • Fixed • Air sign

A quarius is the eleventh and penultimate sign of the
Zodiac and, like the Air which is its element,
subjects are freedom-loving, independent and
communicative. Humanitarian, idealistic and possessing
a keen intellect with a strong sense of justice, Aquarians
enjoy social interaction and the kinship of their fellows.

Planetary Influence

Cold, barren Uranus, ruler of Aquarius, is the planet of change, unpredictability and the intellect. Aquarius, with its inherent dualism, reflects the aspects of both Uranus and its former, 'ancient' ruler, Saturn – characterised by English composer Gustav Holst in his Planets Suite as the 'bringer of old age'. Saturn imposes limitations, an awareness of responsibilities and represents the father figure seeking to discipline his child for its own good. Unstable, changeable Uranus, radical and freedom-loving, grants Aquarians an individualistic, progressive outlook which may be seen as a sense of 'vision'. Leaders and reformers are often born under this sign.

Positive traits
Independent, freedom-loving, humanitarian and with a clarity of 'vision' which is often light years ahead of their time, gregarious Aquarians are happiest in social groups where their charming, individualistic approach often means that they are leading lights in their particular social spheres. Inventive and with finely balanced powers of reasoning, clear-sighted Aquarians may use their progressive thinking to change and reform conditions for their fellows. Aquarians are loyal to partners and friends.

Negative traits
In pursuit of their own dreams, Aquarians can become blind to all else, being fanatical and even dangerously single-minded in this respect. Their natural inventiveness and originality may be construed as eccentricity and their truthful outspokenness may decline into boorish tactlessness. The influence of Uranus may cause the crusading Aquarian to be erratic, stubborn, rebellious and inconsistent. The influence of Saturn can create over-conscientiousness, isolation and depression when goals are not achieved.

January

1905 Christian Dior, French couturier, b. Granville

21

1788 Lord Byron, English poet, b. London

22

1832 Edouard Manet, French artist, b. Paris

23

1941 Neil Diamond, American singer and songwriter, b. Brooklyn, New York

24

1759 Robert Burns, Scottish poet, b. Alloway, Ayrshire

25

1925 Paul Newman, American film actor, b. Cleveland, Ohio

26

1756 Wolfgang Amadeus Mozart, Austrian composer, b. Salzburg

27

Since the comparatively modern designation of Uranus to Aquarius, flight has been linked with this sign. Strangely prophetic was the Greek myth which told of Aquarius depicted as the youth Ganymede who, on the orders of Zeus, was carried to heaven by a great Eagle.

Sense of 'Self'
Aquarians take their awareness of self from society, identifying the interests of the group as their own. Key phrase: 'I am the embodiment of all that society needs or desires.'

The Mythology of Aquarius

Reflecting the sign's duality, the symbol of Aquarius is the Water Carrier or the God with Two Streams. The Egyptian zodiacal image symbolises Hapi, the Nile God – offering life-giving flows of water to mankind. Held by some to be divine wisdom poured out for the good of humanity, medieval astrologers told of the double flow accompanied by twelve stars as being the 'mystical dew of alchemists'. In Greek mythology, Aquarius was depicted as Ganymede, a beautiful youth who, at the command of Zeus, was carried to heaven by a great eagle, to become cup-bearer to the Olympian Gods.

Ruling planet: Uranus
Uranus was discovered by William Herschel in 1781 and its glyph incorporates the letter 'H' surmounted on the two curves of the soul with a cross in between. Formerly named after its discoverer, the personality of Uranus is typified by the words change, revolution, disruption *and* unpredictability. *In Greek mythology, Uranus was both the son and husband of Earth Goddess Gaia and father of the Titans. He was castrated with a flint sickle by his son, Chronos.*

Ancient ruling planet: Saturn
In medieval astrology, Saturn was the ruler of Aquarius and known as an agricultural God carrying the sickle as a tool of his labour. Saturn still bears his sickle, but this is now known as a destructive implement. Bringing age and wisdom, limitation, self-discipline and a sense of responsibility, Saturn can be a hard taskmaster. He is identified with Chronos, the Greek God of Time, the son of Uranus and the father of Zeus. (See also Capricorn section).

January

1887 Artur Rubinstein, Polish concert pianist, b. Lodz

28

1879 W.C. Fields, American comedy actor, b. Philadelphia, Pennsylvania

29

1937 Vanessa Redgrave, English film and stage actress, b. London

30

1885 Anna Pavlova, Russian prima ballerina b. St. Petersburg

31

Traditional associations of Aquarius
Gemstone: Aquamarine
Metal: Uranium and aluminium
Colours: Aquamarine, turquoise and
* electric blue*
Animal: Large, far-flying birds
Cities: Moscow, St. Petersburg,
* Hamburg and Salzburg*
Countries: Russia, Sweden, Ethiopia
* and Poland*

Lucky for Aquarians
Day: Saturday
Number: Four

Aquarius is anciently linked with the
period when the River Nile in Egypt
begins to overflow – hence the sign's
early connections with Hapi, the Nile
God.

Relationships

Compatible signs: Libra and Gemini
Polar (opposite) sign: Leo
*The Aquarian's detachment, coolness and need for
freedom to pursue his or her own interests is not
conducive to easy, close relationships. Fellow Air signs
Libra and Gemini will respond to this equation each in
their individual way. Libra's ability to 'communicate'
with partners could bring understanding and tolerance
to rebellious Aquarians. Harmony and relationships are
Libran keywords and this partner could be outgoing,
romantic and loving. Receptive, communicative,
flirtatious Gemini has an adaptable quality, bringing a
welcome warmth to the Aquarian lack of emotionality.
Aquarians are faithful and loyal.*

Careers

*Careers requiring inventiveness
and originality of thought are
particularly apt for the Aquarian,
and those with a
'communications' aspect often
appeal. In the radio, television
and computer fields, Air sign
Aquarians can make good
technicians. At best when
working conditions are not
restricted, the Aquarian makes
an excellent aviator, astronomer,
astrologer, scientist, writer or
actor. Careers concerned with
helping others also suit the
Aquarian.*

Health

*The Aquarian is susceptible to
illnesses connected with the
circulatory system – such as
varicose veins, hardening of the
arteries, nerve and blood
disorders. (Their opposite sign,
Leo, is concerned with the heart
which is dependent upon good
circulation for its correct
functioning). Ankles and shins
are particularly vulnerable parts
of the body and care should be
taken with regard to breaks,
fractures and sprains in these
areas. Toothache and pyorrhoea
are other possible ailments.*

February

1901 Clark Gable, American film actor, b. Cadiz, Ohio

1 SYLA 1977

1650 Nell Gwyn, English actress and mistress of King Charles II, b. London

2

1809 Felix Mendelssohn, German composer, b. Hamburg

3

1902 Charles Lindbergh, American aviator, b. Detroit, Michigan

4

1788 Sir Robert Peel, English Prime Minister and founder of the Metropolitan Police Force, b. Bury, Lancashire

5

1564 Christopher Marlowe, English poet and dramatist, b. Canterbury, Kent

6

1812 Charles Dickens, English novelist, b. Portsmouth, Hampshire

7

'Crystalline brother of the belt of
  heaven,
Aquarius ! to whom King Jove has
  given
Two liquid pulse-streams 'stead
  of feathered wings.'
John Keats, Endymion, *Book IV*

Gemstone: Aquamarine

The aquamarine is a pale blue to greenish-blue transparent variety of beryl and represents water in the mineral kingdom. It was said that a person's familiar spirit could be invoked by looking into the polished surface of this gemstone and, as a consequence, aquamarines were worn by those wishing to know the innermost secrets of others. Closely related to the aquamarine is the emerald, often represented as the Eye of Horus of ancient Egyptian myth. The Eye of Horus is said to be placed invisibly in the Aquarian forehead and is symbolic of the sign's sense of inner vision.

Known from Roman times as the 'life-force' crystal, and said to reflect the colour of Earth as seen from space, ancient healers and soothsayers used the aquamarine to assess a person's aura or 'life-force'.

Once thought to be the solidified tears of sea-sirens, aquamarines were said to have the power to cure watery and itchy eyes, swollen hands, stomach upsets, varicose veins, and to strengthen the legs and enhance foot health.

1828 Jules Verne, French novelist and early exponent of the science fiction genre, b. Nantes

8

1945 Mia Farrow, American film actress, b. Los Angeles, California

9

1890 Boris Pasternak, Russian author, b. Moscow

10

1934 Mary Quant, English fashion designer, b. London

11

1809 Charles Darwin, English naturalist, b. Shrewsbury, Shropshire

12

1903 Georges Simenon, Belgian author and creator of Maigret, b. Liège

13

1894 Jack Benny, American comedian, b. Chicago, Illinois

14

February

1564 Galileo Galilei, Italian astronomer and physicist, b. Pisa

15

1959 John McEnroe, American tennis champion, b. Wiesbaden, Germany

16

1941 Gene Pitney, American singer and songwriter, b. Hartford, Connecticut

17

1894 Andrés Segovia, Spanish classical guitarist, b. Linares

18 EILEEN

Flowers and trees

Flowers
Apple blossom: Fame
Lemon blossom: Fidelity in love
Peach blossom: I am your captive
Elder flowers: Zealousness
Orchid: Beauty
Trees
Cherry: Good education
Plum: Keep your promises
Fig: Prolific
Others
Zestful citrus fruits such as lemon and lime. Peppers, chillies, herbs and spices with sharp, distinctive flavours.

Pisces

19th February – 20th March

A Feminine • Negative • Mutable • Water sign

*P*isces is the twelfth and last sign of the Zodiac. With implications of hidden depths, Water sign Pisceans are mystical, imaginative, peace-loving people with a need for privacy and possessing a strong spiritual sensitivity. Deeply intuitive and often influenced by spiritualism and the occult, Pisceans are natural psychics and mediums.

Planetary Influence

The great Sea God Neptune is the ruling planet of Pisces whose duality is symbolised by two fishes swimming in opposite directions yet bound together by a 'silver cord'. Neptune brings a nebulous aspect to this sign, creating a mystical personality which, in reaching for the intangible, is often drawn to religion – not necessarily orthodox – to discover its inner self. 'Ancient' ruler Jupiter also has a religious dimension, granting Pisces the expansion of consciousness, aspirations and spiritual development characteristic of the sign. Bountiful Jupiter brings maturity and growth to Pisces while Neptune, symbolising hidden depths, cultivates detachment and a strong desire for privacy.

Positive traits
Pisceans are caring, sensitive people, making intuitive and sympathetic listeners. They are full of understanding and forgiveness and have an empathy with, and are kind to, animals. Capable of acts of great self-sacrifice, receptive to the emotions of others, happy, peace-loving and convivial by nature, Pisceans are charming companions. Intelligent and in a creative sense, inspired, having perceptive powers of interpretation, Pisceans can be pure idealists who enjoy supporting good causes.

Negative traits
Difficulty in making decisions and concentrating on practical matters can cause the Piscean to drift ineffectually. Due to hypersensitivity, they may also suffer from mood swings, guilt complexes and an inability to express themselves clearly. Procrastination is inherent to the Piscean nature, and self-discipline in this respect may be necessary. Dwelling in a Neptunian dream world often means that Pisceans resort to alcohol and drugs to fulfil their need for emotional and mental stimulation.

February

1843 Adelina Patti, Italian opera singer, b. Madrid, Spain	19
1927 Sidney Poitier, American film actor, b. Miami, Florida	20
1728 Peter III, Tsar of Russia and grandson of Peter the Great, b. Kiev, Ukraine	21
1908 Sir John Mills, British film actor, b. Felixstowe, Suffolk	22
1685 George Frideric Handel, German composer, b. Halle, Saxony	23
1786 Wilhelm Grimm, German collector of fairy tales, b. Hanau	24
1841 Pierre Auguste Renoir, French painter, b. Limoges	25

A Greek legend recalls that where Orpheus laid his lute upon a mossy bank, there the first violet grew. Another legend has it that the violet has only dropped its head since the shadow of the Cross fell on it at the crucifixion of Christ.

'Smooth runs the water where the brook is deep'
William Shakespeare, Henry VI Pt 2, Act iii, Sc. 1

The Mythology of Pisces

Roman mythology recalls how Venus and Cupid were chased by Typhon, leapt into the Euphrates and were saved by two fishes. Granted a place in the heavens by the grateful Goddess, these were known thereafter as The Fishes. The Piscean mysteries have long had intimate links with the church and the dawn of the Age of Pisces saw the birth of Christ and the development of Christianity. The Fish became the secret symbol of Christ, a symbolism embodied in the ritual of baptism by water. Perhaps with astrological significance, Jesus chose disciples whom He called the Fishers of Men.

Ruling planet: Neptune

The discovery of Neptune by Johann Galle on 23rd September 1846 occurred because astronomers observed its strange gravitational influence on Uranus, which caused that planet to move erratically in its orbit. Coinciding with the emergence of Spiritualism and such esoteric practices as hypnotism and mesmerism, Neptune became known as The Mystic. The Roman equivalent of Poseidon, Greek God of the Sea, Neptune was married to Amphitrite. Bringing intuitiveness and idealism, Neptune is associated with super-consciousness and spiritual development.

Ancient ruling planet: Jupiter

The God Jupiter or 'Jove' was the most important and powerful God in the Roman pantheon. The counterpart of the Greek God Zeus and deemed to be the Father of the Gods, Jupiter was the son of Saturn (Chronos) whose throne he usurped. Largest of all the planets and considered by astrologers to be the most benevolent, Jupiter, known as the 'Great Benefic', brings expansiveness, joviality and grants the reward of material growth when plans mature. (See also Sagittarius section).

February

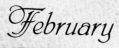

1802 Victor Hugo, French novelist, b. Besancon

26

1932 Elizabeth Taylor, English film actress, b. London

27

1910 Vincente Minelli, American film producer, b. Chicago, Illinois

28

1904 Jimmy Dorsey, American musician and bandleader, b. Shenandoah, Pennsylvania

29

Traditional associations of Pisces
Gemstone: Amethyst
Metal: Germanium and strontium
Colours: Mauve, purple and violet,
 sea green and silver
Animal: Sea-loving mammals and all
 fish
Cities: Hollywood, Alexandria,
 Warsaw and Jerusalem
Countries: Portugal, many small
 Mediterranean islands, the Gobi
 and Sahara deserts and
 Scandinavia

Lucky for Pisceans
Day: Thursday
Number: Seven

Sense of 'Self'
Self-sacrificial Pisceans surrender all
to a higher, mystical Being.
Key phrase: 'I am in harmony, in
unison with the mysteries of the
Universe.'

Relationships

Compatible signs: Cancer and Scorpio
Polar (opposite) sign: Virgo
Dreamy Pisces, poetic and lyrical in love seeks always to discover the fairy tale romance. Sensitive, maternal and protective Cancer offers a warm, affectionate romance. A perceptive and intuitive understanding could enrich this relationship. Passionate and mystically emotional, Scorpios hold a magnetic attraction for Pisceans. However, woe betide the little Fish who incurs the wrath of a jealous, vindictive Scorpio partner. With a warmth and a genuine desire to make others happy, Pisceans require a caring, loving yet forceful partner to counterbalance the Neptunian muddled vagueness in financial and practical issues.

Careers

All careers connected with the sea are appropriate for the Piscean. Also those concerning the arts – specifically the dance which reflects the rhythm of the sea – or acting, writing poetry or prose, painting or sculpture. The 'caring' professions – minister of religion, social worker, nurse, doctor, masseur – all are appropriate to the sympathetic Piscean. Particularly apt professions for this intuitive, perceptive sign are those of medium, psychic or diviner.

Health

Pisces rules the feet, the liver, clotting mechanisms and blood circulation. Conditions affecting feet and toes, such as bunions, corns and gout prevail – also cirrhosis of the liver where there has been an excessive intake of alcohol. Illnesses connected with nervous stress and allergies to certain drugs are common. Care should be taken with regard to contaminated water and seafood. Pisces also rules the pituitary gland which controls the flow and cycle of the body.

March

1810 Fréderic-François Chopin, Polish composer, b. Zelazowa Wola

1

1931 Mikhail Gorbachev, Russian statesman, b. Stravropol

2

1911 Jean Harlow, American film actress, b. Kansas City, Kansas

3

1923 Patrick Moore, English astronomer, b. Pinner, Middlesex

4

1908 Rex Harrison, English actor, b. Liverpool

5

1475 Michelangelo Buonarotti, Italian artist, b. Tuscany

6

1792 Sir John Herschel, English astronomer and son of Sir William Herschel, b. Slough, Buckinghamshire

7

Iris, the Greek Goddess of the Rainbow – so named because of the numbers of colours that this bloom can have – was the bearer of good tidings to mortals. Hence the meaning attached to the flower: I have a message for you.

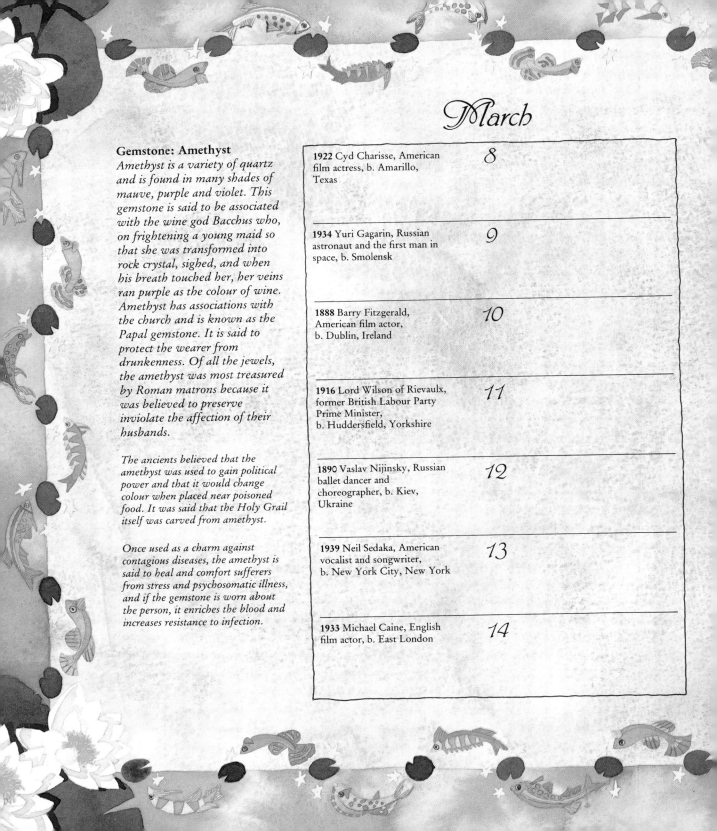

March

Gemstone: Amethyst

Amethyst is a variety of quartz and is found in many shades of mauve, purple and violet. This gemstone is said to be associated with the wine god Bacchus who, on frightening a young maid so that she was transformed into rock crystal, sighed, and when his breath touched her, her veins ran purple as the colour of wine. Amethyst has associations with the church and is known as the Papal gemstone. It is said to protect the wearer from drunkenness. Of all the jewels, the amethyst was most treasured by Roman matrons because it was believed to preserve inviolate the affection of their husbands.

The ancients believed that the amethyst was used to gain political power and that it would change colour when placed near poisoned food. It was said that the Holy Grail itself was carved from amethyst.

Once used as a charm against contagious diseases, the amethyst is said to heal and comfort sufferers from stress and psychosomatic illness, and if the gemstone is worn about the person, it enriches the blood and increases resistance to infection.

1922 Cyd Charisse, American film actress, b. Amarillo, Texas

8

1934 Yuri Gagarin, Russian astronaut and the first man in space, b. Smolensk

9

1888 Barry Fitzgerald, American film actor, b. Dublin, Ireland

10

1916 Lord Wilson of Rievaulx, former British Labour Party Prime Minister, b. Huddersfield, Yorkshire

11

1890 Vaslav Nijinsky, Russian ballet dancer and choreographer, b. Kiev, Ukraine

12

1939 Neil Sedaka, American vocalist and songwriter, b. New York City, New York

13

1933 Michael Caine, English film actor, b. East London

14

March

1916 Harry James, American band leader and trumpeter, b. Albany, Georgia

15

1926 Jerry Lewis, American comedy actor, b. Newark, New Jersey

16

1938 Rudolf Nureyev, Russian ballet dancer, b. Irkutsk, Siberia

17

1844 Nikolai Rimsky-Korsakov, Russian composer, b. Tikhvin, Novgorod

18

1936 Ursula Andress, Swiss film actress, b. Berne

19

1917 Dame Vera Lynn, British singer and World War II 'Forces Favourite', b. London

20

Flowers and trees

Flowers
Iris: I have a message for you
Orchid: Beauty
Water lily: Purity of heart
Angelica: Inspiration
Violet: Modesty
Trees
Weeping willow: Mourning
All trees growing by water
Fig: Prolific
Others
Foods with a high water content – such as cucumber, water melon and lettuce

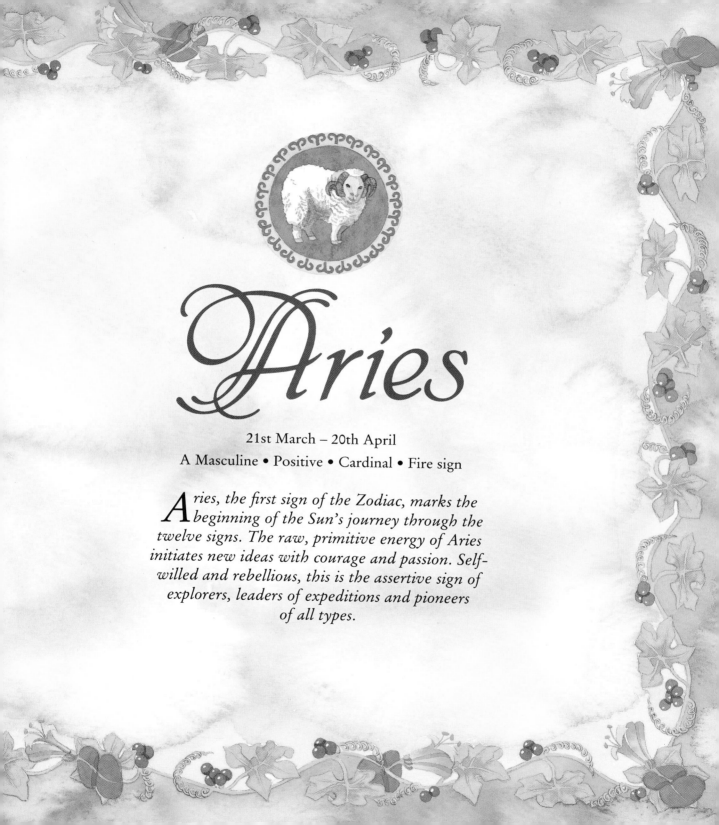

Aries

21st March – 20th April

A Masculine • Positive • Cardinal • Fire sign

*A*ries, the first sign of the Zodiac, marks the
beginning of the Sun's journey through the
twelve signs. The raw, primitive energy of Aries
initiates new ideas with courage and passion. Self-
willed and rebellious, this is the assertive sign of
explorers, leaders of expeditions and pioneers
of all types.

Planetary Influence

Mars, the Roman God of War, signifies initiative and energy, pioneering instincts, leadership and passion. The traits of this planet are almost identical to those of Aries and are, therefore, intensified. Primarily, Mars brings a strong desire for leadership, expressed with courage and assertiveness. Self-willed Aries is rarely able to restrain from acting on impulse, but with underlying reasons which are generally sound. Fiery Aries has little concern with the inadvisability of such actions – it is sufficient that self-expression has been achieved. A close sign-ruler association give impetus to Aries' ego energy and a 'me first' assertiveness typifies this sign.

Positive traits

Arians are direct in manner and speech and do not tolerate subterfuge and duplicity. They can be stimulating, if sometimes tactless, companions, being incisive and satirical in their conversation. Enterprising and showing unlimited energy when dealing with their own affairs, Arians 'think on their feet' and react well under stress. While displays of fiery anger are quick to flare, these fade just as swiftly as they break out initially: Arians do not tend to harbour long-term resentment.

Negative traits

The forcefulness and drive of Aries, if misused, can degenerate into selfish, aggressive and quarrelsome behaviour which displays a complete disregard for the feelings of others. The egocentric Aries can be imprudent, boastful and show a restlessness often resulting in impulsive, foolhardy heroics. Careerwise, promotion of self, and a tendency to progress at the expense of others, can be seen as ruthlessness. Positive channelling of the Martian energy drive is essential to Arians.

March

1685 Johann Sebastian Bach, German composer, b. Eisenach
21

1923 Marcel Marceau, French mime artist, b. Strasbourg
22

1908 Joan Crawford, American film actress, b. San Antonio, Texas
23

1930 Steve McQueen, American film actor, b. Indianapolis, Indiana
24

1947 Elton John, British composer and singer, b. Pinner, Middlesex
25

1911 Tennessee Williams, American playwright, b. Columbus, Mississippi
26

1863 Sir Frederick Henry Royce, English car manufacturer, b. Alwalton, Huntingdonshire
27

Sense of 'Self'
The raw, unharnessed energy of Aries seeks fulfilment of self on its own assertively primitive terms. Key phrase: 'I am first. I want to be first. I will be first. I am first.'

'At last from Aries rolls the bounteous sun.'
James Thomson, The Seasons, Spring

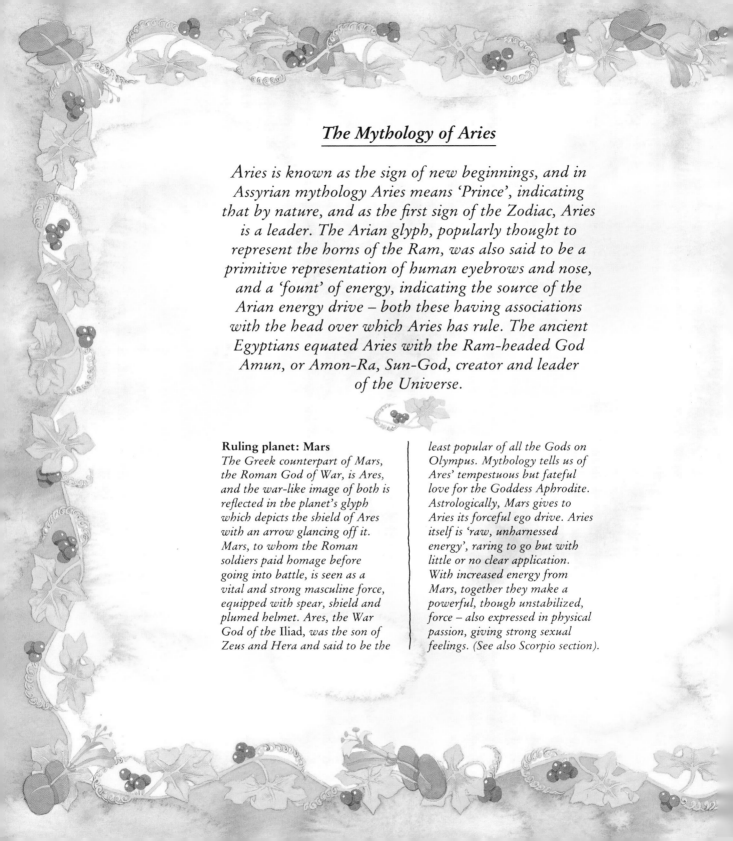

The Mythology of Aries

Aries is known as the sign of new beginnings, and in Assyrian mythology Aries means 'Prince', indicating that by nature, and as the first sign of the Zodiac, Aries is a leader. The Arian glyph, popularly thought to represent the horns of the Ram, was also said to be a primitive representation of human eyebrows and nose, and a 'fount' of energy, indicating the source of the Arian energy drive – both these having associations with the head over which Aries has rule. The ancient Egyptians equated Aries with the Ram-headed God Amun, or Amon-Ra, Sun-God, creator and leader of the Universe.

Ruling planet: Mars

The Greek counterpart of Mars, the Roman God of War, is Ares, and the war-like image of both is reflected in the planet's glyph which depicts the shield of Ares with an arrow glancing off it. Mars, to whom the Roman soldiers paid homage before going into battle, is seen as a vital and strong masculine force, equipped with spear, shield and plumed helmet. Ares, the War God of the Iliad, was the son of Zeus and Hera and said to be the least popular of all the Gods on Olympus. Mythology tells us of Ares' tempestuous but fateful love for the Goddess Aphrodite. Astrologically, Mars gives to Aries its forceful ego drive. Aries itself is 'raw, unharnessed energy', raring to go but with little or no clear application. With increased energy from Mars, together they make a powerful, though unstabilized, force – also expressed in physical passion, giving strong sexual feelings. (See also Scorpio section).

March

1483 Raphael Santi, Italian artist, b. Urbino

28

1869 Sir Edwin Lutyens, English architect, b. London

29

1853 Vincent van Gogh, Dutch artist, b. Groot-Zundert

30

1872 Sergei Diaghilev, Russian ballet impresario, b. Novgorod

31

Traditional associations of Aries
Gemstone: Diamond
Metal: Iron
Colours: Red, scarlet and carmine
Animal: Ram
Cities: Florence, Verona, Naples and
*   Marseilles*
Countries: France, Germany,
*   England and Denmark*

Lucky for Arians
Day: Tuesday
Number: Nine

Maypoles were often made of hawthorn, a tree symbolising joy at the return of Summer and traditionally associated with Aries. The hawthorn was also used as a wreath for the Green Man who represented the Spirit of the Woods.

Relationships

Compatible signs: Leo and Sagittarius
Polar (opposite) sign: Libra
For impulsive Aries, life is motivated by an assertive ego drive which tolerant Leo could harness and stabilise with warm-hearted kindliness. Each has the forceful sexuality associated with all the Fire signs, and Leo's generous affections should be amply rewarded by passionate Aries! The third Fire sign, jovial, expansive Sagittarius could bring bonhomie, optimism and intellectual stimulation to a partnership with Aries, who should be fully prepared to allow freedom-loving Sagittarius plenty of rein. Arians are ardent, though generally faithful and can make possessive, even jealous, partners who require understanding.

Careers

Careers presenting a challenge appeal most to Arians – especially those where energy and initiative are required, such as racing driver, sportsman, member of the armed services or explorer. As Aries rules the head, Arians often make good hair stylists, or – on the mental plane – psychiatrists and psychologists. Associations with fire and metal make the blacksmith and steelworker obvious choices – also professions which involve cutting tools. And, given the incisive Arian wit – a writer of satire!

Health

Diseases that 'head-first' Arians should guard against are conditions associated with the head – such as those affecting the brain, the face and eyes, the upper jaw, the cerebrum and carotid arteries. Typical Arian complaints are brain fever due to stress and overwork, headaches, neuralgic and eye troubles, toothache and gumboils – also feverish illnesses, such as influenza. Accidents to the head, resulting in blood loss, and cuts and burns reflect the red, caustic influence of Mars.

April

1932 Debbie Reynolds, American film actress and singer, b. El Paso, Texas

1

1840 Emile Zola, French novelist, b. Paris

2

1924 Marlon Brando, American film actor, b. Omaha, Nebraska

3

1934 Anthony Perkins, American film actor, b. New York City

4

1908 Bette Davis, American film actress, b. Lowell, Massachusetts

5

1929 André Previn, American composer and conductor, b. Berlin, Germany

6

1915 Billie Holiday, American jazz and blues singer, b. Baltimore, Maryland

7

' . . . and these men of Mars causeth warre and batayle . . . They will gladly be workers of yron . . . red and angry and a maker of swordes and knyves . . .'
Compost of Ptolomeus

Gemstone: Diamond

The diamond, with its brilliant lustre is nature's hardest known mineral. It is said to ensure longevity, and, to quote from the Boke of Secrets of Albertus Magnus, *if bound to one's left side, the diamond is 'good against enemies, madness, wild beasts . . . against chiding men, . . . venom and the invasion of fantasies.' Legends surrounding the great diamonds of history – such as the Koh-i-Noor, the Hope and the Orloff Diamond – abound, and most concern the disastrous influence of this fateful jewel. Much prized and often of value beyond the dreams of avarice, the diamond remains the most coveted and desirable of all known jewels.*

The ancient Romans believed that the diamond warded off madness, bolstered courage and ensured long life for its owner. More practically, before splitting a diamond, Roman craftsmen dipped it in goat's blood 'to make it fragile'.

The diamond has always been a token of love – its purity and durability symbolising the qualities of that love. Also known as the Philosophers' Stone, alchemists believed the diamond to be the ultimate in beauty and perfection.

April

1889 Sir Adrian Boult, English conductor, b. Chester — **8**

1806 Isambard Kingdom Brunel, English engineer, b. Portsmouth — **9**

1932 Omar Sharif, Egyptian film actor, b. Alexandria — **10**

1819 Sir Charles Hallé, English founder of the Hallé Orchestra, b. Hagen, Germany — **11**

1941 Bobby Moore, English international footballer, b. London — **12**

1917 Howard Keel, American singer and actor, b. Gillespie, Illinois — **13**

1925 Rod Steiger, American film actor, b. Westhampton, New York — **14**

April

1894 Bessie Smith, American blues singer, b. Chattanooga, Tennessee

15

1921 Sir Peter Ustinov, English actor and writer, b. London

16

1918 William Holden, American film actor, b. O'Fallon, Illinois

17

Flowers and trees

Flowers

Anemone: Forsaken

Honeysuckle: Generous and devoted affection

Thistle: Retaliation

Peppermint: Warmth of feeling

Bryony: Artful deception

Trees

Hawthorn: Hope

Evergreen thorn: Solace in adversity

Spruce: Hope in adversity

Others

Most strong-tasting foods such as onions, leeks, hops and capers. Hot spices associated with Aries are mustard and cayenne pepper.

1480 Lucrezia Borgia, Italian noblewoman, b. Rome

18

1932 Jayne Mansfield, American film actress, b. Bryn Mawr, Pennsylvania

19

1808 Napoleon III, Emperor of France, b. Paris

20

Taurus

21st April – 21st May

A Feminine • Negative • Fixed • Earth sign

Taurus, the second sign of the Zodiac signifies stage two in the development of the ego – symbolically it is the awareness of the young child of others, and its desire for warm, secure relationships. Nature-loving, down-to-earth Taurus is cautious, mindful of possessions and enjoys good food and wine.

Planetary Influence

If the Aries ego definition is 'me' – then Taurus's is 'mine'. For Taurus is a patient, plodding, steadfast individual for whom physical possessions hold a very real significance. The favourable and warming influence of Venus brings charm and romance to rugged Taurus who, without her friendly beneficence, would be much less amenable and agreeable. 'Earthy' Taureans, with their strong Earth-connectedness, enjoy Nature and outdoor pursuits – a characteristic often expressed in their love of gardens and all things growing. The Goddess of Love brings a companionable warmth to this sign, bestowing upon it a love of the arts and good food and wine.

Positive traits

Taureans make loyal, steadfast companions and are caring and protective towards loved ones and possessions. They are practical and competent in the management of business affairs and prefer a stable, organised routine, disliking new projects or ventures. Taureans enjoy cultural pursuits, often being talented in an artistic field – and since Taurus rules the throat, many are blessed with good speaking or singing voices. Dedicated bons vivants and lovers of luxury, Taureans make charming, hospitable hosts.

Negative traits

The plodding 'down-to-earth' Taurean can become too 'fixed' and stubborn in attitude, placing too much significance on conservatism. He or she may lack imagination and show obstinacy with a tendency to boorishness. Inertia and indolence in the workplace, selfishness, avarice and meanness can become evident. The Venusian love of luxury may succumb to over-indulgence causing weight problems. The Taurean's inbuilt awareness of possessions can become overstressed, creating jealousy and suspicion.

April

1926 Queen Elizabeth II of England, b. London   *21*

1916 Sir Yehudi Menuhin, British violinist, b. New York City   *22*

1564 William Shakespeare, English playwright and poet, b. Stratford-on-Avon   *23*

1934 Shirley Maclaine, American film actress and dancer, b. Richmond, Virginia   *24*

1873 Walter de la Mare, English novelist and poet, b. Charlton, Kent   *25*

1452 Leonardo da Vinci, Italian artist, b. Vinci   *26*

1904 Cecil Day Lewis, English author and Poet Laureate, b. Sligo, Ireland   *27*

'Venus loveth ryot and dispense.'
Geoffrey Chaucer, The Canterbury Tales, 6, 282

Venus in medieval astrology 'signfyeth white men or browne . . . joyfull laughter, liberall pleasures, dancers, entertayners of women, players, perfumers, musicians, messengers of Love . . .'
Anon

The Mythology of Taurus

Taurus, the Heavenly Bull, whose earliest known name in Persian astrology meant the 'Bull of Light', is also seen as demi-Taurus, with hindquarters which are lost in the clouds, and as the mer-bull (Taurus with a fish tail), an example of magical imagery signifying the sign's spirituality. Linked with the sacred Bull of Mithraism and Apis, another celestial bull, Taurus represented the Egyptian sacred Bull within whose body the God Osiris was incarnate. To the Egyptians, Taurus, who symbolised fertility and growth, indicated the time for ploughing the Earth. There were associations too with the Greek God Zeus who, taking the form of a bull, abducted the mortal girl Europa.

Ruling planet: Venus

Venus, the Goddess of Love, signifies beauty, sensuality and a love of art and music. Also, not only is there a desire for erotic, physical love in the Taurean nature, but also a need for warmth and affection and a yearning to bestow these qualities. Venus brings to Taurus a love of the luxuries in life and a desire to possess beautiful things. Symbolising harmony, unison and relatedness, Venus is said to govern that period of adolescence when a person begins to attract, and is attracted by, the opposite sex. This is also a time when relationships are formed and possessions are gathered. The glyph of Venus depicts the Circle of Spirit surmounted by, and having precedence over, the Cross of Matter. The Greek counterpart of Venus is Aphrodite, so named because she sprang from the foam of the sea (Gr: aphros, foam) and mythology recalls that whoever wore Aphrodite's magic girdle became the object of love. (See also Libra section).

April

1878 Lionel Barrymore, American film actor, b. Philadelphia, Pennsylvania

28

1863 William Randolph Hearst, American newspaper publisher, b. San Francisco, California

29

1870 Franz Lehár, Hungarian composer, b. Komarón

30

'The rose looks fair, but fairer we it deem
For that sweet odour, which doth in it live'
William Shakespeare, Sonnet 54

Sense of 'Self'
Earth-bound Taurus identifies with the fecundity, the 'passiveness' of warm soil.
Key phrase: 'I give stability, steadfastly; value possessions, protectively, and indulge in earthy pleasures, sensually.'

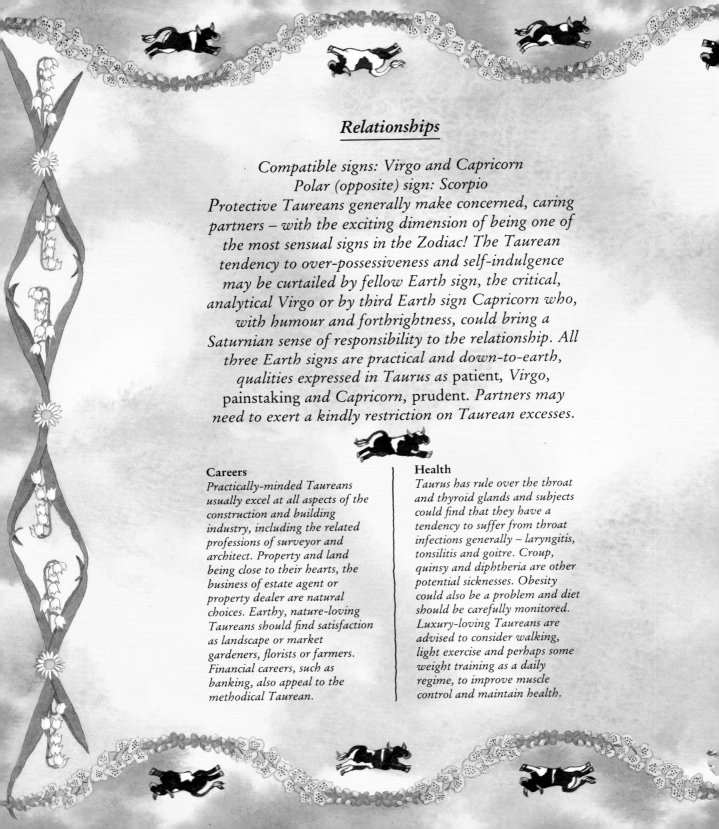

Relationships

Compatible signs: Virgo and Capricorn
Polar (opposite) sign: Scorpio

Protective Taureans generally make concerned, caring partners – with the exciting dimension of being one of the most sensual signs in the Zodiac! The Taurean tendency to over-possessiveness and self-indulgence may be curtailed by fellow Earth sign, the critical, analytical Virgo or by third Earth sign Capricorn who, with humour and forthrightness, could bring a Saturnian sense of responsibility to the relationship. All three Earth signs are practical and down-to-earth, qualities expressed in Taurus as patient, Virgo, painstaking and Capricorn, prudent. Partners may need to exert a kindly restriction on Taurean excesses.

Careers

Practically-minded Taureans usually excel at all aspects of the construction and building industry, including the related professions of surveyor and architect. Property and land being close to their hearts, the business of estate agent or property dealer are natural choices. Earthy, nature-loving Taureans should find satisfaction as landscape or market gardeners, florists or farmers. Financial careers, such as banking, also appeal to the methodical Taurean.

Health

Taurus has rule over the throat and thyroid glands and subjects could find that they have a tendency to suffer from throat infections generally – laryngitis, tonsilitis and goitre. Croup, quinsy and diphtheria are other potential sicknesses. Obesity could also be a problem and diet should be carefully monitored. Luxury-loving Taureans are advised to consider walking, light exercise and perhaps some weight training as a daily regime, to improve muscle control and maintain health.

May

1916 Glenn Ford, film actor, b. Quebec, Canada

1

1892 Baron Manfred von Richthofen, German air ace in World War I, b. Prussia

2

1920 Sugar Ray Robinson, American boxer, b. Detroit, Michigan

3

1929 Audrey Hepburn, English film and stage actress, b. Brussels, Belgium

4

1818 Karl Marx, German philosopher and the 'Father of Communism', b. Trier

5

1915 Orson Welles, American actor, director and producer, b. Kenosha, Wisconsin

6

1812 Robert Browning, English poet, b. Camberwell, London

7

Traditional associations of Taurus
Gemstone: Emerald
Metal: Copper
Colours: Pale blue, yellow, pink and
  pale green
Animal: Bull – and all other cattle
Cities: Dublin, Lucerne, Palermo
  and St. Louis
Countries: Ireland, Switzerland,
  Cyprus and the Greek Islands

Lucky for Taureans
Day: Friday
Number: Six

May

Gemstone: Emerald

The rich, green emerald, which enjoys a fascinating history, was said to be a link with divine forces and have associations with the eye. Effigies of Gods and Goddesses may be seen with eyes of this gemstone and one instance is that of the mythological Eye of Horus, the ancient Egyptian God. The jewel of the Goddess Venus, typifying the transmission of vital forces and used in rites to incite love and passion, the emerald was thought to ensure perpetual fertility. Practitioners in the ancient art of crystal healing use the emerald to relieve pain during childbirth, as an antidote to poison and to improve the memory.

In ancient Egypt the emerald symbolised resurrection and was worn to achieve a favourable reincarnation. Egyptian legend also has it that 'if a Serpent fixes its eye on this jewel, it will become blind.'

In the lore of crystal healing, the emerald is said to cure diseases of the eye. The emerald is also said to be effective in relieving stress, high blood pressure, skin ulcers, food poisoning and headaches.

1926 Sir David Attenborough, English naturalist and broadcaster, b. Cambridge

8

1873 Howard Carter, English Egyptologist, b. Swaffham, Norfolk

9

1899 Fred Astaire, dancer and film actor, b. Omaha, Nebraska

10

1888 Irving Berlin, American composer, b. Tyumen, E. Russia

11

1812 Edward Lear, English poet and artist, b. Highgate, London

12

1950 Stevie Wonder, American composer and singer, b. Saginaw, Michigan

13

1727 Thomas Gainsborough, English artist b. Sudbury, Suffolk

14

May

1859 Pierre Curie, French physicist, b. Paris

15

1919 Liberace, American pianist and entertainer, b. West Allis, Wisconsin

16

1911 Maureen O'Sullivan, Irish film actress, b. Bayle

17

1919 Dame Margot Fonteyn, English prima ballerina, b. Reigate, Surrey

18

1861 Dame Nellie Melba, Australian opera singer, b. Melbourne

19

1799 Honoré de Balzac, French novelist, b. Tours

20

1916 Harold Robbins, American novelist, b. New York

21

Flowers and trees

Flowers
Narcissus: Egotism
Lily of the Valley: Return of
  happiness
Foxglove: Insincerity
Rose: Love
Poppy: Fantastic extravagance
Trees
Fig: Prolific
Vine: Intoxication
Apple: Temptation
Others
Wheat and most other cereals,
  grapes, apples, pears,
  artichokes, asparagus and most
  spices are associated with
  Taurus.

Gemini

22nd May – 21st June

A Masculine • Positive • Mutable • Air sign

Third sign of the Zodiac, Gemini is one half of the positive-negative pair of signs in which the mental and emotional aspects of the archetypal individual are developing. Gemini is the 'mental' part of this duo. Inquisitive, intelligent, restless and adaptable, Air sign Gemini excels in the communications field.

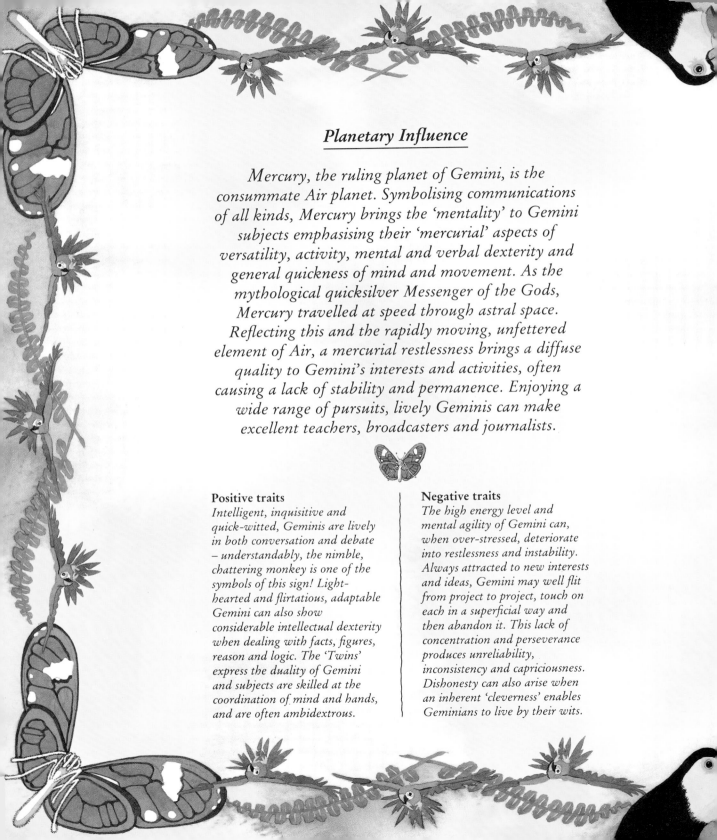

Planetary Influence

Mercury, the ruling planet of Gemini, is the consummate Air planet. Symbolising communications of all kinds, Mercury brings the 'mentality' to Gemini subjects emphasising their 'mercurial' aspects of versatility, activity, mental and verbal dexterity and general quickness of mind and movement. As the mythological quicksilver Messenger of the Gods, Mercury travelled at speed through astral space. Reflecting this and the rapidly moving, unfettered element of Air, a mercurial restlessness brings a diffuse quality to Gemini's interests and activities, often causing a lack of stability and permanence. Enjoying a wide range of pursuits, lively Geminis can make excellent teachers, broadcasters and journalists.

Positive traits

Intelligent, inquisitive and quick-witted, Geminis are lively in both conversation and debate – understandably, the nimble, chattering monkey is one of the symbols of this sign! Light-hearted and flirtatious, adaptable Gemini can also show considerable intellectual dexterity when dealing with facts, figures, reason and logic. The 'Twins' express the duality of Gemini and subjects are skilled at the coordination of mind and hands, and are often ambidextrous.

Negative traits

The high energy level and mental agility of Gemini can, when over-stressed, deteriorate into restlessness and instability. Always attracted to new interests and ideas, Gemini may well flit from project to project, touch on each in a superficial way and then abandon it. This lack of concentration and perseverance produces unreliability, inconsistency and capriciousness. Dishonesty can also arise when an inherent 'cleverness' enables Geminians to live by their wits.

May

1907 Sir Laurence Olivier, English actor, b. Dorking, Surrey

22

1910 Artie Shaw, American bandleader and clarinettist, b. New York

23

1819 Queen Victoria b. Kensington Palace, London

24

1879 Lord Beaverbrook, British statesman and newspaper owner, b. Ontario, Canada

25

1920 Peggy Lee, American singer, b. Jamestown, South Dakota

26

1878 Isadora Duncan, American dancer, b. San Francisco, California

27

1908 Ian Fleming, English novelist, b. London

28

The Roman God Mercury, whose planet rules Gemini, has associations with commerce and is sometimes shown with coins or a purse. Mercury is the source of the words market, merchant and merchandise.

Sense of 'Self'
Mentally-orientated Gemini has a constantly questing, never-resting intellectual drive.
Key phrase: 'On the wings of the wind and with the swiftness of sound, I encircle the Earth . . .'

The Mythology of Gemini

Gemini is symbolised by the Celestial Twins who, in Greek mythology, were Castor and Pollux, twin sons of Leda and Zeus. Castor was seen as the mortal and Pollux as the immortal twin and when Castor was slain, leaving behind a grief-stricken Pollux, Zeus, out of fatherly concern for his sons, made both immortal and placed them in the Heavens. Gemini, from the Latin meaning twin, has been variously interpreted throughout the ages – one of these interpretations seeing them as Man and Woman. Folklore sees in Gemini the duality of nature: growth and decay, light and dark, summer and winter.

Ruling planet: Mercury

In Roman mythology, Mercury was the son of Jupiter and Maia. The equivalent of the Greek God Hermes, wind deity Mercury was deemed the messenger of the Gods, and was sacred to commerce and science, and known as the patron of merchants – also of rogues, vagabonds, thieves and travellers! On 15th May, the Roman festival of Mercury was held and merchants would sprinkle themselves and their wares with water to ensure prosperity. Portrayed as a youth in winged helmet and sandals, Mercury carries a caduceus: a winged staff sometimes seen as comprising two snakes entwined. Mercury is associated with a 'silver tongue' or eloquence and this is seen in its astrological sign Gemini, whose subjects are noted for their quickness of wit and eloquence. The glyph of Mercury represents the half circle of human spirit surmounting the Circle of Divine Spirit, with the Cross of earthly Matter below. (See also Virgo section).

May

1903 Bob Hope, American film actor and comedian, b. Eltham, London

29

1909 Benny Goodman, American bandleader and clarinettist, b. Chicago, Illinois

30

1923 Prince Rainier III, reigning head of the House of Grimaldi, b. Monaco

31

Traditional associations of Gemini
Gemstone: Agate
Metal: Quicksilver
Colours: Yellow, slate grey and
spotted mixtures
Animal: Parrots and other brightly
coloured birds, monkeys and
butterflies
Cities: London, San Francisco,
Cordoba and Bruges
Countries: Belgium, USA, Sardinia
and Armenia

Lucky for Geminians
Day: Wednesday
Number: Five

Relationships

Compatible signs: Libra and Aquarius
Polar (opposite) sign: Sagittarius
The Air signs tend to be less passionate than other signs
and, as such, Air sign Gemini is flirtatious and enjoys
light-hearted affairs. While the appropriate partner
could inspire them to love quite deeply, Geminis tend
to have more than one significant relationship in their
lives. Fellow Air signs Libra and Aquarius share
Gemini's intellect and both would bring a keen sense of
justice and a restraint to Gemini's inconstancies. Libra
would bring balance and a 'hesitancy'; Aquarius,
reasoning and a social awareness. Partners should not
be too concerned about Gemini's roving eye!

Careers

Geminis excel at all types of communication and in particular those occupations which allow their initiative and imagination free expression. Making ideal journalists, broadcasters and authors, they are also accomplished linguists, translators, teachers, lecturers and salespeople, occupations that give Gemini's agile mental and verbal skills full expression. Careers connected with travel i.e. war correspondent, news reporter, courier, dispatch rider, travel agent – or aerobatics pilot – are all typically 'mercurial'.

Health

Gemini has rule over the hands, arms, lungs and nervous system and this restless sign suffers health difficulties with these parts of the body. Respiratory and nervous disorders, however, are the main Geminian health problems. Counterbalancing nervous excitability, periods of rest are advisable and a channelling of Gemini's compulsive restlessness will avoid debilitating exhaustion. Overcoming illnesses comparatively quickly, Geminis keep a youthful appearance throughout their lives.

June

1926 Marilyn Monroe, American film actress, b. Los Angeles, California

1

1840 Thomas Hardy, English poet and novelist, b. Upper Bockhampton, Dorset

2

1925 Tony Curtis, American film actor, b. New York City

3

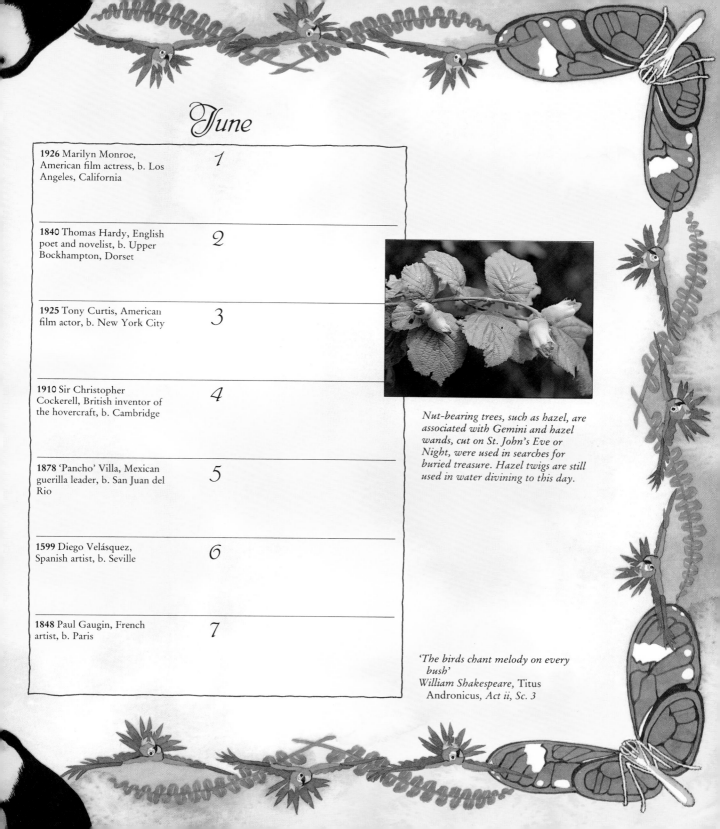

1910 Sir Christopher Cockerell, British inventor of the hovercraft, b. Cambridge

4

Nut-bearing trees, such as hazel, are associated with Gemini and hazel wands, cut on St. John's Eve or Night, were used in searches for buried treasure. Hazel twigs are still used in water divining to this day.

1878 'Pancho' Villa, Mexican guerilla leader, b. San Juan del Rio

5

1599 Diego Velásquez, Spanish artist, b. Seville

6

1848 Paul Gaugin, French artist, b. Paris

7

'The birds chant melody on every bush'
William Shakespeare, Titus Andronicus, Act ii, Sc. 3

June

Gemstone: Agate

Agate, a coloured, opaque relation of chalcedony, has been known for thousands of years. Throughout the ages agates with varying patterns and colours had such exotic names as ogle-eye, ribbon, star, coral and the spotted agate. The moss agate, so named for its delicate dark green 'leaf' pattern, was a talisman for farmers and an aid to water divining – attributed then to Venus in her role as Goddess of Fertility. The Sumerians of Mesopotamia used these precious stones to protect themselves and to improve their crops. Astrologically, the agate is now associated with Mercury, the ruler of Gemini.

The name agate came from the River Achates, or Gagates, in Sicily where, long ago, Roman soldiers found the smooth, round pebbles and kept them as talismans to ward off evil and to bring good fortune.

Agate was said to render a person invisible, and to turn the swords of foes against themselves. Shakespeare's Mercutio in Romeo and Juliet also speaks of Queen Mab as being 'no bigger than an agate-stone on the forefinger of an alderman'.

1810 Robert Schumann, German composer, b. Zwickau

8

1891 Cole Porter, American composer and lyricist, b. Peru, Indiana

9 ?WIESIA GROCHOCKI

1921 Prince Philip, Duke of Edinburgh, b. Corfu, Greece

10

1864 Richard Strauss, German composer, b. Munich

11

1924 George Bush, 41st President of the USA, b. Milton, Massachusetts

12

1893 Dorothy L. Sayers, English writer of detective stories, b. Oxford

13

1928 Ernesto 'Che' Guevara, Argentinian revolutionary, b. Rosario

14

June

1843 Edvard Grieg,
Norwegian composer,
b. Bergen

15

1890 Stan Laurel, English
comic film actor,
b. Ulverstone, Lancashire

16

1703 John Wesley, English
preacher and founder of the
Methodist movement,
b. Epworth, Lincolnshire

17

1942 Paul McCartney,
member of The Beatles, b.
Liverpool

18

1919 Louis Jourdain, French
film actor, b. Marseilles

19

1909 Errol Flynn, American
film actor, b. Hobart,
Tasmania

20

1905 Jean-Paul Sartre, French
author and dramatist, b. Paris

21

Flowers and trees
Flowers
Lavender: Distrust
Blue violet: Faithfulness
*Lily-of-the-Valley: Return of
 happiness*
Fern: Fascination
Trees
Hazel: Reconciliation
Chestnut: Do me justice, luxury
All nut-bearing trees
Others
*Nuts and all vegetables grown
 above the ground, except
 cabbage, are foods associated
 with Gemini, as are such herbs
 and spices as marjoram,
 caraway and aniseed.*

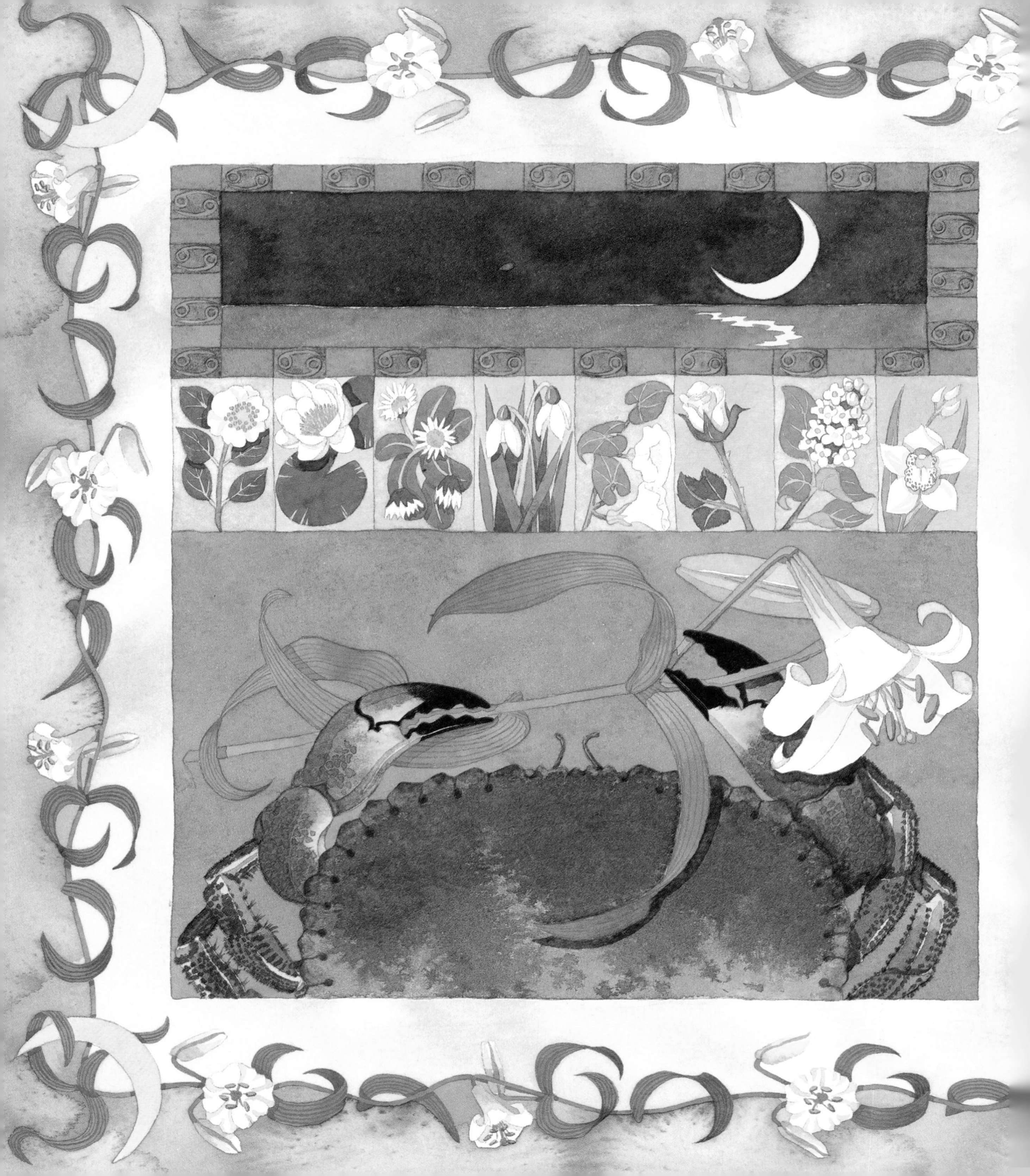

Cancer

22nd June – 22nd July

A Feminine • Negative • Cardinal • Water sign

The fourth sign of the Zodiac is Cancer, the second and 'emotional' half of the Gemini/Cancer positive-negative duo. Fundamentally, Cancer requires emotional security and has a strong mother-connectedness with the desire to nurture and nourish. Cancerians are home-loving, intuitive, sensitive and relate happily to the 'caring' professions.

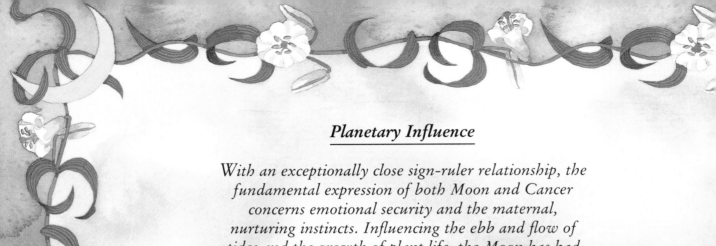

Planetary Influence

With an exceptionally close sign-ruler relationship, the fundamental expression of both Moon and Cancer concerns emotional security and the maternal, nurturing instincts. Influencing the ebb and flow of tides and the growth of plant life, the Moon has had irrevocable links with fertility and motherhood since the dawn of Time. The Moon exerts a powerful influence over her astrological sign and this is reflected in Cancerian mood changes, emotionality, intuitiveness and receptiveness. Governing subconscious reactions and feelings, the Moon brings to Cancer strong, emotional links with the past and a reluctance to break away from home and loved ones.

Positive traits
Affectionate and with a kindly good humour, Cancerians are devoted to home and family and remain loyal to their friends, clinging to failing relationships which would have been abandoned by others. At their best in an environment where their protective and nurturing instincts are allowed free expression, Cancerians are natural 'collectors' and show great tenacity and perseverance – setting and achieving goals with a quiet determination. They are also thrifty and methodical in their business affairs.

Negative traits
The mood changes of Moon-influenced Cancer, subject to the fluctuating phases of their planet, can become exaggerated with hypersensitivity, sentimentalism and self-pity often prevailing. Concern for loved ones may be expressed as fussiness and, if fearful of losing a loved one, Cancer can resort to childish behaviour, becoming possessive and tenaciously clinging. Kindness may swiftly change to 'crabbiness' and a disinclination to discard anything of sentimental value, often leads to a reputation for untidiness!

June

1856 Sir Henry Rider Haggard, English author, b. Bradenham Hall, Norfolk	22
1763 Empress Joséphine, wife of Napoleon Bonaparte, b. Martinique	23
1895 Jack Dempsey, American world heavyweight boxing champion, b. Manassa, Colorado	24
1903 George Orwell, English novelist, b. Motihari, Bengal	25
1904 Peter Lorre, Hungarian film actor, b. Rosenberg	26
1880 Helen Keller, American writer and lecturer, b. Tuscumbia, Alabama	27
1491 King Henry VIII of England, b. Greenwich, London	28

Sense of 'Self'
The Cancerian awareness is of a relationship with the past . . . its childhood, family and especially, mother.
Key phrase: 'I will make secure my home; nourish and nurture my loved ones and protect all, tenaciously.'

The Mythology of Cancer

Cancer is strongly connected with conception and birth. Its glyph is said to represent the male and female seed, the phallic symbol of horizontal 'nines', or the claws of the Crab. Cancer has the greatest number of fixed stars within its arc and many geniuses have been born when their Sun or Ascendent is in Cancer with fixed stars prominent. In Roman mythology, Juno set Cancer against Hercules when he fought the Hydra of Lerna. Cancer bit the foot of the hero who straightaway killed it. Juno then placed Cancer in the Heavens, making it one of the twelve Zodiacal signs.

Ruling planet: The Moon
As the Sun symbolises Fatherhood, so the Moon is Motherhood incarnate. The Sun is Fire; the Moon is Water. Worshipped as goddess and enchantress, her phases were signified thus: as the New Moon, she was the White Goddess of birth and growth; at Full Moon, the Red Goddess of love and war, and when Old, she was the Black Goddess of divination and death. Each month, with virginity renewed, the Moon embodies life's cycle, governing our subconscious reactions and feelings. Reflecting the powerful light of the Sun, the Moon's ever-changing phases are echoed by the tides and, in human life, by the feminine rhythms. The Moon's glyph depicts a crescent Moon or two semi-circles – part reflections of the power of Spirit. In Greek mythology, the Moon was named Hecate before rising and setting, and Astarte when a crescent. To the Romans, she was Diana; to the Greeks, Artemis.

June

1901 Nelson Eddy, American
film actor and singer,
b. Providence, Rhode Island

29

1917 Lena Horne, American
singer, b. Brooklyn, New
York

30

Traditional associations of Cancer
Gemstone: Moonstone and pearl
Metal: Silver
Colours: White, opal, iridescent
  silvery hues, smoky grey, sea green
  and blue
Animal: Crab and other shell-
  covered creatures
Cities: Amsterdam, New York,
  Istanbul and Tokyo
Countries: Scotland, Holland, New
  Zealand and Paraguay

Lucky for Cancerians
Day: Monday
Number: Two

Cancer, ruled by the Moon, has been
known as the Gate of Birth,
signifying the descending journey of
an unborn baby's spirit through the
sphere of the Moon. At death, the
spirit ascends that same sphere to
reach the planetary space thought to
be Heaven.

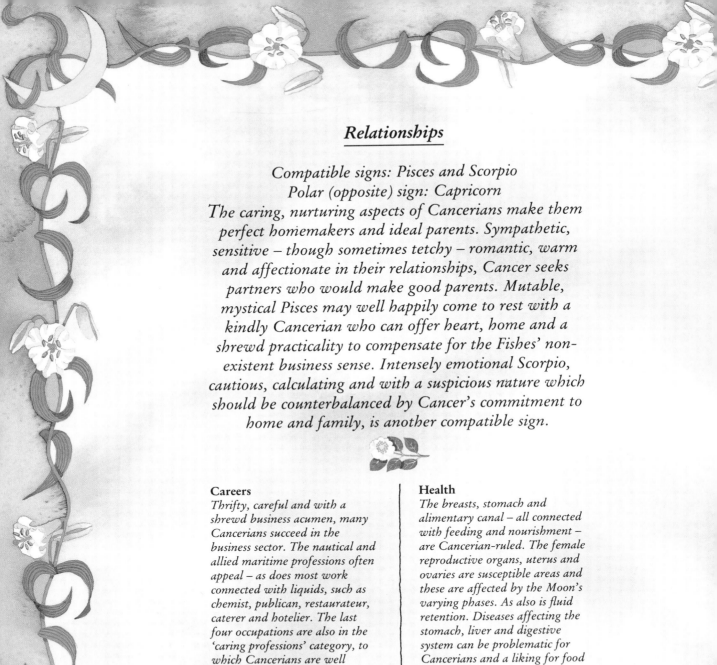

Relationships

Compatible signs: Pisces and Scorpio
Polar (opposite) sign: Capricorn
The caring, nurturing aspects of Cancerians make them
perfect homemakers and ideal parents. Sympathetic,
sensitive – though sometimes tetchy – romantic, warm
and affectionate in their relationships, Cancer seeks
partners who would make good parents. Mutable,
mystical Pisces may well happily come to rest with a
kindly Cancerian who can offer heart, home and a
shrewd practicality to compensate for the Fishes' non-
existent business sense. Intensely emotional Scorpio,
cautious, calculating and with a suspicious nature which
should be counterbalanced by Cancer's commitment to
home and family, is another compatible sign.

Careers
Thrifty, careful and with a
shrewd business acumen, many
Cancerians succeed in the
business sector. The nautical and
allied maritime professions often
appeal – as does most work
connected with liquids, such as
chemist, publican, restaurateur,
caterer and hotelier. The last
four occupations are also in the
'caring professions' category, to
which Cancerians are well
suited. Avid 'collectors',
Cancerians often become
curators or antique dealers.

Health
The breasts, stomach and
alimentary canal – all connected
with feeding and nourishment –
are Cancerian-ruled. The female
reproductive organs, uterus and
ovaries are susceptible areas and
these are affected by the Moon's
varying phases. As also is fluid
retention. Diseases affecting the
stomach, liver and digestive
system can be problematic for
Cancerians and a liking for food
and drink may result in gastric
ulcers – plus the necessity for diet
and exercise!

July

1804 George Sand, French woman writer, b. Paris

1

1489 Thomas Cranmer, Archbishop of Canterbury, b. Aslockton, Nottinghamshire

2

1927 Ken Russell, English film director, b. Southampton

3

1927 Gina Lollobrigida, Italian film actress, b. Subiaco

4

1810 P. T. Barnum, American showman, b. Bethel, Connecticut

5

1937 Vladimir Ashkenazy, Russian pianist and conductor, b. Gorky

6

1940 Ringo Starr, English drummer in The Beatles, b. Liverpool

7

Sir Thomas Gresham, when dining with his Queen, Elizabeth the First, melted a pearl of great value, and drank to her health: ' . . . Instead of sugar, Gresham drinks the Pearl unto his Queen and Mistress'
Thomas Heywood

'To gild refined gold, to paint the lily, Is wasteful and ridiculous excess'
William Shakespeare, King John, Act iv, Sc. 2

July

Gemstones: Moonstone and pearl

The moonstone and the pearl are traditionally associated with the Moon – the moonstone bearing a likeness to its namesake and the pearl symbolising its purity. Adularia, the most precious variety of moonstone, was said to cure lovesick women and epilepsy, and have an uplifting effect when worn by those with a predominant Moon in their chart. The pearl, iridescent gem of the sea, is linked to the Moon because of the planet's influence over tide and sea, and over women, whose rhythmic cycle corresponds to the lunar cycle. Pearls are frequently worn during ceremonial invocations of lunar forces, involving astral activity.

In the past, moonstones were often used for curing lunacy. Their lustre – the moonstone's most healing quality – was said to reflect the wearer's negative, as well as positive, emotions and can therefore be a mixed blessing!

The pearl is said to represent sweet simplicity and the embodiment of feminine innocence. Rich in gemstone lore, Persian mythology maintains that when drops of spring rain fall on to the pearl oyster, they produce pearls.

1839 John D. Rockefeller, American industrialist, b. Richford, New York **8**

1888 Simon Marks, British retail tycoon, b. Leeds **9**

1945 Virginia Wade, English tennis champion, b. Bournemouth **10**

1274 Robert the Bruce, King of Scotland, b. Turnberry, Ayrshire **11**

1730 Josiah Wedgwood, English pottery manufacturer, b. Burslem, Staffordshire **12**

1942 Harrison Ford, American film actor, b. Chicago, Illinois **13**

1858 Emmeline Pankhurst, English suffragette, b. Manchester **14**

July

1606 Rembrandt van Rijn, Dutch artist, b. Leyden

15

1723 Sir Joshua Reynolds, English painter, b. Plympton, Devon

16

1899 James Cagney, American film actor and dancer, b. New York City

17

1848 W. G. Grace, English cricketer, b. Downend, nr. Bristol

18

1834 Edgar Degas, French Impressionist painter, b. Paris

19

1919 Sir Edmund Hillary, New Zealand mountaineer and first conqueror of Mount Everest, b. Auckland

20

1899 Ernest Hemingway, American writer, b. Oak Park, Illinois

21/22

1822 Gregor Mendel, monk, botanist and geneticist, b. Odrau, Austrian Silesia

Flowers and trees

Flowers
White lily: Purity and modesty
White rose: I am worthy of you
Convolvulus: Bonds
Water lily: Purity of heart
All white flowers
Trees
All trees, particularly those rich
  in sap
Others
Milk, fish, fruits and vegetables
  with a high water content,
  white and red cabbage and
  herbs such as verbena and
  tarragon are all linked with
  Cancer.

Leo

23rd July – 23rd August

A Masculine • Positive • Fixed • Fire sign

In Leo, fifth sign of the Zodiac, the individual is complete in all but one aspect – a dependency upon the acknowledgment of others. Sun sign Leo, regal, charismatic and with a strong desire for self-expression, lives life dominating centre stage, playing lead roles with whole-hearted enthusiasm and sincerity.

Planetary Influence

Recognised as the source of all life, symbol of fatherhood and ruler of Leo, the Sun brings to its sign a powerful regality, vitality and whole-heartedness. Leo, the 'King of Beasts', is a natural leader, acting with pride and dignity. Sunny-natured and affectionate, Leo craves appreciation and, as the Sun's reflected rays bring light to the planets, so Leo desires to be a leading light in whose rays others bask and reflect. The Sun, supreme Creative Force, brings to Leo creativity, a love of drama, pomp and pageantry. This is the sign of actors, producers and impresarios.

Positive traits

The positive Leo is bold, courageous, open-minded and has a strong sense of dignity. Born leaders with a generous breadth of vision and excellent organisational skills, the commanding Leonine presence is eminently suited to positions of importance and authority. Leo's generosity, warmth and affection is genuine and their confident, extrovert, 'larger than life' manner makes them greatly admired. Loyal to partners and friends, Leos are optimistic, stout-hearted people, often showing great strength of character.

Negative traits

A personal sense of regality, if over-stressed, may incline an autocratic Leo towards profligacy, arrogance and a pompous, overbearing attitude. An unwillingness to take 'second place' is an extension of their vanity and conceit and whether they are magnanimous 'kings of the castle' or caring heads of the family, Leos expect, as their due, a 'lion's share' of appreciation and adulation. If this is not forthcoming, condescending Leos can be scathing and crushingly dismissive. Lack of fulfilment or repeated assault on leonine dignity may cause depression.

July

1888 Raymond Chandler, American novelist, b. Chicago, Illinois	23
1898 Amelia Earhart, American aviator, b. Atchison, Texas	24
1954 Walter Payton, American football star, b. Columbia, Mississippi	25
1856 George Bernard Shaw, Irish playwright, b. Dublin	26
1870 Hilaire Belloc, English author and poet, b. St. Cloud, France	27
1866 Beatrix Potter, English writer and illustrator, b. London	28
1887 Sigmund Romberg, Hungarian composer, b. Szeged	29

'Small curs are not regarded when
*   they grin,*
But great men tremble when the
*   Lion roars'*
William Shakespeare, Henry VI
*   Pt. 2, Act iii, Sc. 1*

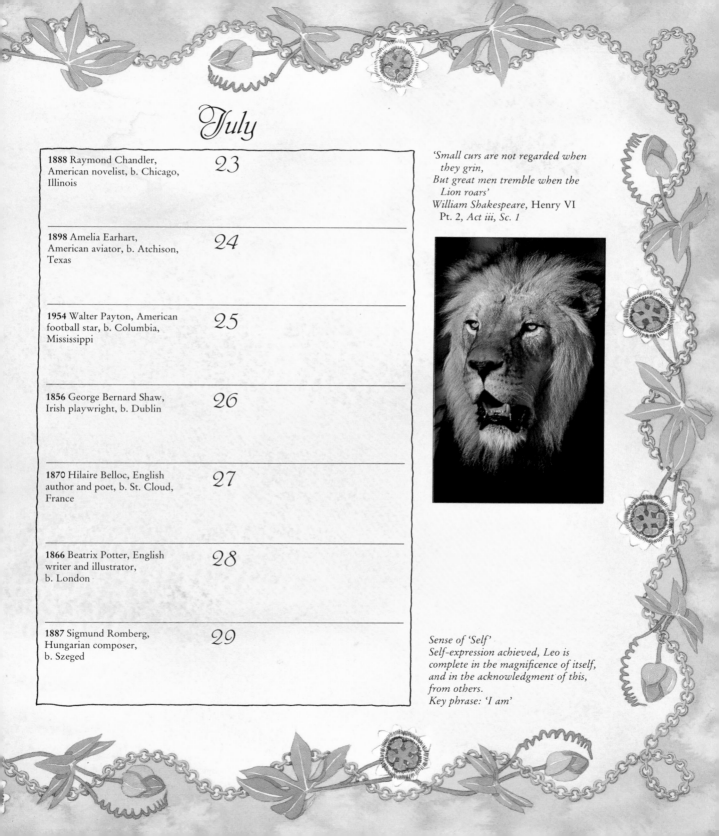

Sense of 'Self'
Self-expression achieved, Leo is
complete in the magnificence of itself,
and in the acknowledgment of this,
from others.
Key phrase: 'I am'

The Mythology of Leo

The Sun sign Leo is associated with the Nemean Lion of Argolis which possessed an impenetrable hide and was strangled by Hercules in the fulfilment of the first of his Twelve Labours. From early times Leo's sign has been symbolised as a Lion – the Babylonians called it the Great Light, and the winged Lion of St. Mark was derived from the Leo of the Babylonian Zodiac. In medieval imagery, Leo was often accompanied by two instruments of kingship, the sceptre and the sword – depicting the capacity for good and evil. 'Leo' said astrologer El Haganah, 'loves the splendour of power . . .'

Ruling planet: The Sun

More than 300,000 times larger than Earth, the fiery Sun generates a continuous output of energy giving heat and light to surrounding planets ranging out from the Sun for some 3,700 million miles. Traversing the Zodiac and spending approximately one month in each sign, the Sun's mystical number is One and it gives its name to Sunday, the first day of our week. Associated with the heart, fatherhood and creativity, Leo's ruler has been worshipped as the source of our being since ancient times. To the Assyrians the Sun was Shamash, to the Persians, Mithras and to the Egyptians, Ra. In Greek mythology, the Sun was Helios, ascending the heavens to bring light to the day and disappearing into the sea in the evening. To the Romans, the Sun was Sol and, later, had associations with Apollo. The Sun's glyph represents the circle of primal life, while the central dot symbolises its seed.

July

1863 Henry Ford, American automobile engineer and industrialist, b. Greenfield, Michigan	*30*
1951 Evonne Goolagong, Australian tennis champion, b. New South Wales	*31*

Traditional associations of Leo
Gemstone: Ruby
Metal: Gold
Colours: Orange, gold, rich shades of
  yellow, brown
Animal: Lion
Cities: Rome, Madrid, Damascus
  and Bombay
Countries: Italy, Sicily, southern Iraq
  and Lebanon

Lucky for Leos
Day: Sunday
Number: One

'O 'tis the Sun that maketh all things
  shine'
William Shakespeare, Love's
  Labour's Lost, Act iv, Sc. 3

Relationships

Compatible signs: Aries and Sagittarius
Polar (opposite) sign: Aquarius
Making a warm, generous and affectionate partner, albeit requiring constant approval and respect from its mate, Leo enjoys and excels in the role of 'patriarch' and provider. Fiery, self-assertive Aries, reacting to Leo's somewhat splendid sense of self, could ignite a passionate flame and bring a headstrong exuberance to a possible relationship. Third Fire sign, the likeable, freedom-loving Sagittarius could add an extrovert vigour to life with Leo – particularly since both have athletic and sporting inclinations. Leos are fiercely loyal to partners and, ideally, an adoring mate would caringly curb Leo's unremitting power drive.

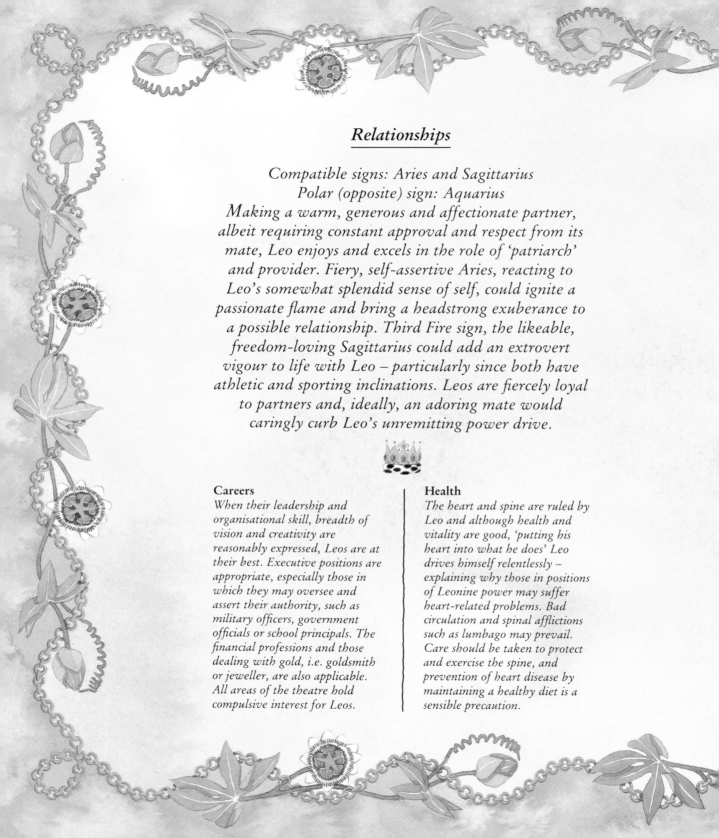

Careers

When their leadership and organisational skill, breadth of vision and creativity are reasonably expressed, Leos are at their best. Executive positions are appropriate, especially those in which they may oversee and assert their authority, such as military officers, government officials or school principals. The financial professions and those dealing with gold, i.e. goldsmith or jeweller, are also applicable. All areas of the theatre hold compulsive interest for Leos.

Health

The heart and spine are ruled by Leo and although health and vitality are good, 'putting his heart into what he does' Leo drives himself relentlessly – explaining why those in positions of Leonine power may suffer heart-related problems. Bad circulation and spinal afflictions such as lumbago may prevail. Care should be taken to protect and exercise the spine, and prevention of heart disease by maintaining a healthy diet is a sensible precaution.

August

1819 Herman Melville, American novelist, b. New York City

1

1925 Alan Whicker, British television broadcaster, b. Cairo, Egypt

2

1938 Terry Wogan, Irish television and radio presenter, b. Limerick

3

1792 Percy Bysshe Shelley, English poet, b. Warnham, Sussex

4

1906 John Huston, American film director, b. Nevada, Missouri

5

1917 Robert Mitchum, American film actor, b. Bridgeport, Connecticut

6

1876 Mata Hari, Dutch courtesan and spy, b. Leeuwarden

7

'A good heart's worth gold'
William Shakespeare, Henry IV,
Pt. 2, Act ii, Sc. 4

August

Gemstone: Ruby

Purplish-red rubies are found in Sri Lanka; but the deeper, richer variety from Burma are considered to be the finest, having a colour described as resembling 'pigeon's blood'. Believed by the ancients to be an antidote to poison, to preserve persons from the plague, repress the ill-effects of luxury and to divert the mind from evil thoughts, the star ruby, above all, is held to be the most magical. Representing the fiery radiance of the Sun and symbolic of that planet's 'creative' energy, the ruby also has associations with blood – astrologically considered to be the vehicle of energy.

When worn on the left side of the body, it is said that the ruby will turn black to warn the wearer of imminent danger – returning to its former rosy hue when that danger has passed.

Burmese legend recalls that there was a great Serpent which produced three eggs. From the first two came the King of Pagan and the Emperor of China. The third contained a magical seed from which grew Burmese rubies.

8 — **1988** Princess Beatrice of York, daughter of the Duke and Duchess of York, b. London

9 — **1938** Rod Laver, Australian tennis player, b. Queensland

10 — **1874** Herbert Hoover, 31st President of the USA, b. West Branch, Iowa

11 — **1897** Enid Blyton, English children's author, b. South London

12 — **1881** Cecil B. de Mille, American film producer, b. Ashfield, Massachusetts

13 — **1899** Alfred Hitchcock, English film director, b. London

14/15 — **1867** John Galsworthy, English playwright and novelist, b. Combe, Surrey — **1771** Sir Walter Scott, Scottish writer and poet, b. Edinburgh

August

1958 Madonna, American singer and actress, b. Bay City, Michigan

16

1892 Mae West, American film actress and sex symbol, b. Brooklyn, New York

17

1933 Roman Polanski, French film director, b. Paris

18

1883 'Coco' Chanel, French couturier, b. nr. Issoire

19

1778 Bernardo O'Higgins, Chilean revolutionary and first president b. Chillán

20

1930 HRH Princess Margaret, b. Glamis Castle, Scotland

21

1862 Claude Debussy, French composer, b. St. Germain-en-Laye, nr. Paris

22/23

1912 Gene Kelly, American film actor and dancer, b. Pittsburgh, Pennsylvania

Flowers and trees
Flowers
Sunflower: Haughtiness
Marigold: Jealousy
Celandine: Joys to come
Passion flower: Religious superstition
Trees
Laurel: Glory
Bay wreath: Reward of merit
Palm: Victory
Walnut: Intellect
Others
Honey, rice and green vegetables with a high iron content such as spinach, kale and watercress are typically Leonine foodstuffs. These also include meat and the herbs rosemary, rue and saffron.

Virgo

24th August – 22nd September

A Feminine • Negative • Mutable • Earth sign

Virgo, the sixth sign of the Zodiac, completes the 'physical' stage in the evolution of the individual. Virgo confronts the personal dimension and also that of society, adapting and coming to terms with these while striving to achieve perfection through self-criticism and self-analysis. Virgo's concern is with order, efficiency and exactitude.

Planetary Influence

*Mercury emphasises the communicative capabilities –
these being less abstract and much more down-to-Earth
in Virgo than in Air sign Gemini. The 'mercurial'
quickness to learn, balanced by the retentiveness of
Earth, means that in Virgo, this learning may be
usefully communicated to others, for instance through
teaching. Predominantly motivated by method and
practicality, critical and analytical Virgo is thought by
some to have an uneasy relationship with Mercury.
Certain aspects, however, are compatible – such as
Mercury's coolness of unfettered air, expressed in Virgo
by detachment and 'virginal' untouchability. Virgoans
are generally industrious and have high standards.*

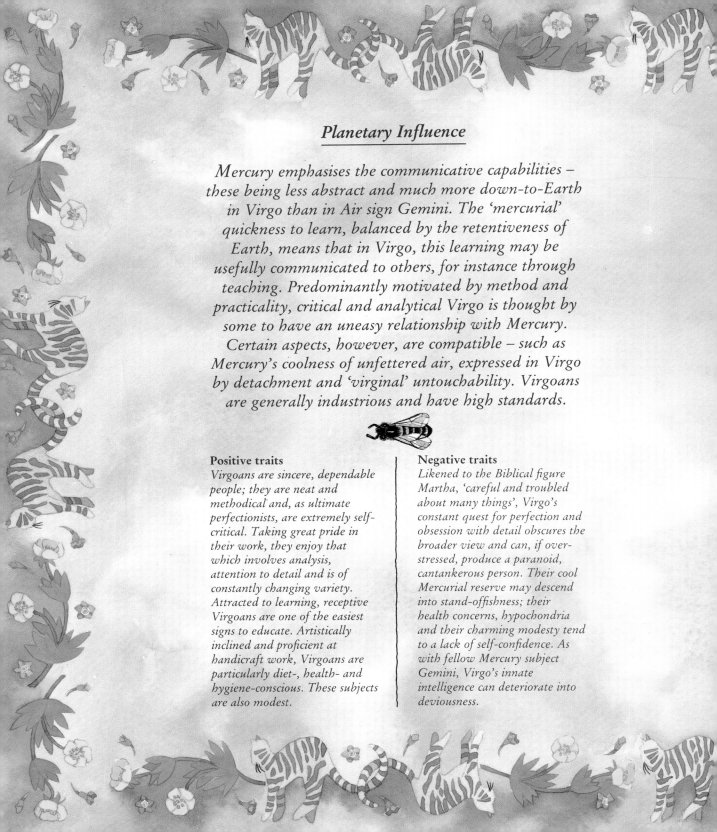

Positive traits
*Virgoans are sincere, dependable
people; they are neat and
methodical and, as ultimate
perfectionists, are extremely self-
critical. Taking great pride in
their work, they enjoy that
which involves analysis,
attention to detail and is of
constantly changing variety.
Attracted to learning, receptive
Virgoans are one of the easiest
signs to educate. Artistically
inclined and proficient at
handicraft work, Virgoans are
particularly diet-, health- and
hygiene-conscious. These subjects
are also modest.*

Negative traits
*Likened to the Biblical figure
Martha, 'careful and troubled
about many things', Virgo's
constant quest for perfection and
obsession with detail obscures the
broader view and can, if over-
stressed, produce a paranoid,
cantankerous person. Their cool
Mercurial reserve may descend
into stand-offishness; their
health concerns, hypochondria
and their charming modesty tend
to a lack of self-confidence. As
with fellow Mercury subject
Gemini, Virgo's innate
intelligence can deteriorate into
deviousness.*

August

1872 Sir Max Beerbohm, English author and caricaturist, b. London

24

As Mercury, the ruling planet of Virgo, was symbolised as the Messenger of the Gods, so were bees in ancient times also regarded as divine messengers. In European lore, people would whisper family news to the hive. If this was not done, it was said that the bees would fly away, never to return.

1918 Leonard Bernstein, American composer and conductor, b. Lawrence, Massachusetts

25

1819 Prince Albert, Consort of Queen Victoria, b. Rosenau, Coburg

26

1882 Samuel Goldwyn, American film producer, b. Warsaw, Poland

27

1828 Count Leo Tolstoy, Russian novelist and philosopher, b. Tula

28

A Virgoan flower, the buttercup represents childhood and can mean 'memories of childhood'. The buttercup can also mean 'ingratitude'.

1915 Ingrid Bergman, Swedish film actress, b. Stockholm

29

1896 Raymond Massey, Canadian film actor, b. Toronto

30/31

1913 Sir Bernard Lovell, English astronomer, b. Oldham Common, Gloucestershire

The Mythology of Virgo

When Astraea, Greek Goddess of justice and last of the deities to leave Earth, ascended to heaven, she became Virgo. Fertility Goddesses and harvest maidens such as Demeter and Ishtar have also represented Virgo, and in Roman mythology Justitia, existing long before man ever sinned, returned to heaven as Virgo, sixth sign of the Zodiac. The Egyptians saw Virgo as Nidaba, Goddess of grain – so named because their harvest began when the Moon was in this constellation. Christianity recognised Virgo as the Virgin Mary and Virgo, clothed in flowing robes, is generally portrayed carrying a wheat sheaf, palm leaves or a vase.

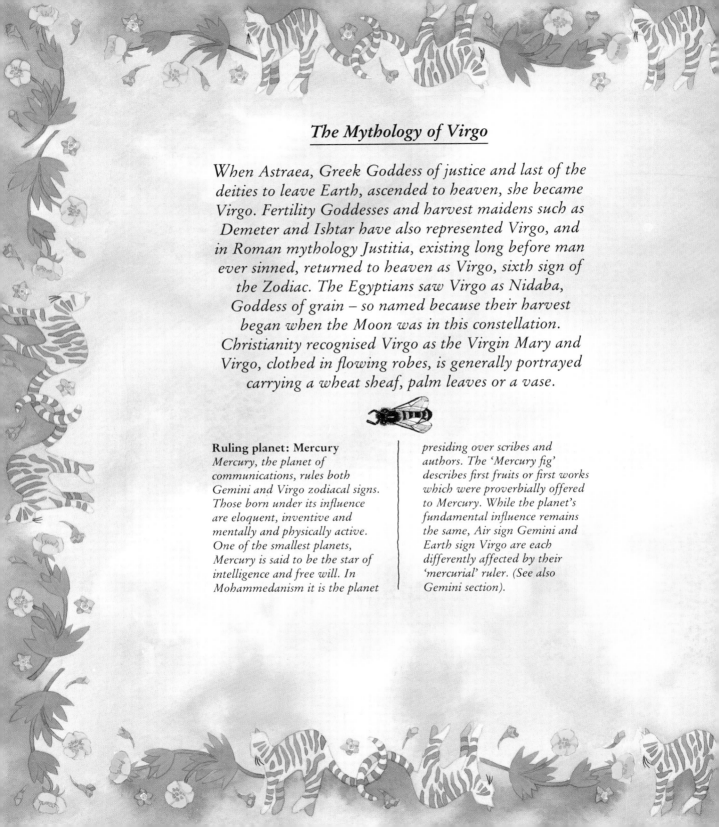

Ruling planet: Mercury
Mercury, the planet of communications, rules both Gemini and Virgo zodiacal signs. Those born under its influence are eloquent, inventive and mentally and physically active. One of the smallest planets, Mercury is said to be the star of intelligence and free will. In Mohammedanism it is the planet presiding over scribes and authors. The 'Mercury fig' describes first fruits or first works which were proverbially offered to Mercury. While the planet's fundamental influence remains the same, Air sign Gemini and Earth sign Virgo are each differently affected by their 'mercurial' ruler. (See also Gemini section).

September

1924 Yvonne de Carlo, American film actress, b. Vancouver, Canada

1

1952 Jimmy Connors, American tennis champion, b. East St. Louis, Illinois

2

1913 Alan Ladd, American film actor, b. Hot Springs, Arkansas

3

1824 Anton Bruckner, Austrian composer, b. Ansfelden

4

1940 Raquel Welch, American film actress, b. Chicago, Illinois

5

1942 Britt Ekland, Swedish film actress, b. Stockholm

6

1936 Buddy Holly, American singer and guitarist, b. Lubbock, Texas

7

As Pisces is said to be linked with Jesus Christ, so Virgo is associated with the Virgin Mary. Astrologically, the relationship can be seen as opposite signs Virgo and Pisces 'constantly regarding each other in adoration'.

Sense of 'Self'
In striving to achieve perfection, so does Virgo gain fulfilment.
Key phrase: 'With attention to detail and with humility, I serve'.

Relationships

Compatible signs: Capricorn and Taurus
Polar (opposite) sign: Pisces
Virgoans make neat, methodical homemakers, always
'on the go', improving their homes with useful,
artistically pleasing items – often crafted by themselves.
Their health and hygiene concerns would be most
acceptable to cautious Capricorn, who would also
admire Virgo's careful handling of financial affairs.
Capricornians make responsible, faithful partners who,
like Virgoans, may also be prone to nervous stress.
Patient, plodding Taurus would bring a warm,
Venusian sensuality to a submissive, 'virginal' Virgo.
Partners need to be accommodating to this critical,
perfectionist sign which constantly demands of the best.

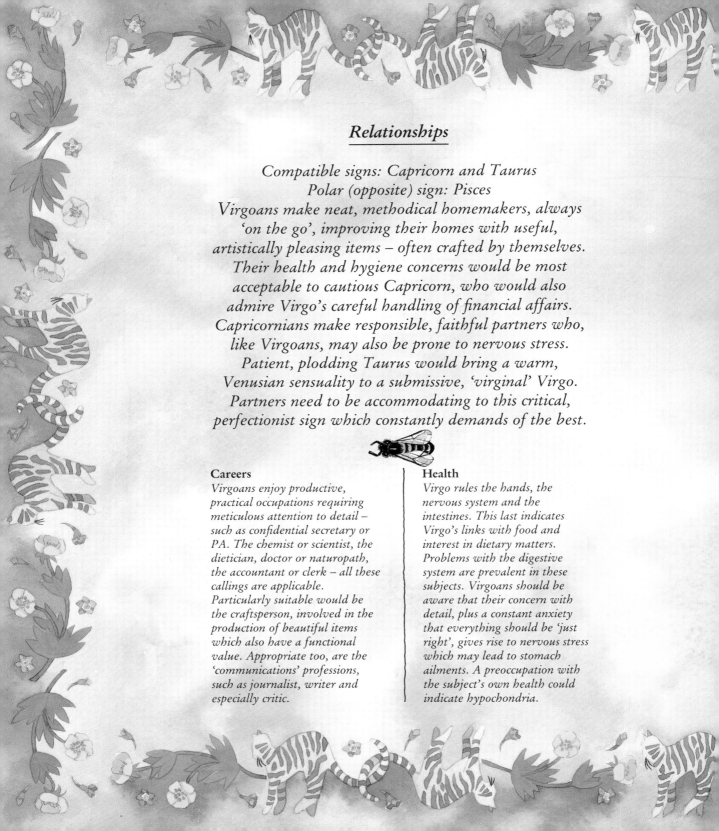

Careers

Virgoans enjoy productive,
practical occupations requiring
meticulous attention to detail –
such as confidential secretary or
P.A. The chemist or scientist, the
dietician, doctor or naturopath,
the accountant or clerk – all these
callings are applicable.
Particularly suitable would be
the craftsperson, involved in the
production of beautiful items
which also have a functional
value. Appropriate too, are the
'communications' professions,
such as journalist, writer and
especially critic.

Health

Virgo rules the hands, the
nervous system and the
intestines. This last indicates
Virgo's links with food and
interest in dietary matters.
Problems with the digestive
system are prevalent in these
subjects. Virgoans should be
aware that their concern with
detail, plus a constant anxiety
that everything should be 'just
right', gives rise to nervous stress
which may lead to stomach
ailments. A preoccupation with
the subject's own health could
indicate hypochondria.

September

1841 Antonin Dvořák, Czech composer, b. nr. Prague

8

1585 Cardinal Richelieu, French statesman, b. nr. Chinon

9

1929 Arnold Palmer, American golfer, b. Latrobe, Pennsylvania

10

1885 D. H. Lawrence, English novelist b. Eastwood, Nottinghamshire

11

1888 Maurice Chevalier, French singer and actor, b. Paris

12

1905 Claudette Colbert, American film actress, b. Paris, France

13

1909 Peter Scott, English naturalist, b. London

14

Traditional associations of Virgo
Gemstone: Sardonyx
Metal: Quicksilver
Colours: Shades of green, dark brown, slate and spotted patterns
Animals: Cats and bees
Cities: Boston, Heidelberg, Paris and Corinth
Countries: Greece, Turkey, Crete and Lower Silesia

Lucky for Virgoans
Day: Wednesday
Number: Five

September

Gemstone: Sardonyx

The gemstone of Virgo is the sardonyx – a variety of chalcedony. It was named 'sard' because it was to be found in the ancient agate-trading centre of Sardis in Asia Minor, and 'onyx' or 'nail' because its colour resembles that of the skin beneath the human nail. As onyx is an agate – an opaque relation of chalcedony – and features black and white banding, so sardonyx is an agate banded with opal, quartz and chalcedony, giving a rich combination of orange, brown and white hues. Chalcedony itself is believed to drive away sadness and protect the wearer from depressing influences, melancholy and 'dark dread . . .'

A gemstone often ornately carved, one exquisite sardonyx cameo (c. 3rd century BC) depicts the Egyptian King Ptolemy II and his daughter who, according to custom, was also his wife. The meaning of sardonyx is Conjugal Felicity.

The sardonyx signifies power and vivacity and, when worn as an amulet, is said to lead to exalted positions, give courage to orators and bashful lovers, protect warriors, preserve the wounded and aid women in childbirth.

1891 Agatha Christie, English crime writer, b. Torquay, Devon

15

1924 Lauren Bacall, American film actress, b. New York City

16

1929 Stirling Moss, British motor racing champion, b. London

17

1905 Greta Garbo, Swedish film actress, b. Stockholm

18

1949 'Twiggy', English model and actress, b. Neasden, London

19

1934 Sophia Loren, Italian actress, b. Naples

20

1931 Larry Hagman, American actor; b. Fort Worth, Texas

21

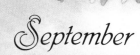

September

1791 Michael Faraday, English scientist, b. Newington Butts, Surrey

22

Flowers and trees

Flowers
Buttercup: Ingratitude
Forget-me-not: True love
Morning Glory: Affectation
Aster: Variety
Mimosa: Sensitiveness
Trees
Hazel: Reconciliation
Horse chestnut: Luxury
All nut-bearing trees
Others
Potatoes, carrots, turnips, swedes and all vegetables grown under the earth. Also nuts of all varieties.

Libra

23rd September – 23rd October

A Masculine • Positive • Cardinal • Air sign

Libra, as the seventh astrological sign, enters the second half of the Zodiac and is desirous of amiable communion on simple terms – as in the one-to-one relationship. Symbolising balanced, harmonious unity with a significant 'other', charming Libra is also the sign of justice, diplomacy and the arts.

Planetary Influence

Subjects of Venus are of pleasing appearance and make charming companions. Special one-to-one and preferably lasting relationships are Libra's fundamental concern, and Venus brings the desire for harmony within these relationships. The Air element imparts the need for communication with that special 'other' so that, together, balanced and harmonious conditions are realised. The significant Venusian sense of, and need for, beauty is a predominant Libran trait. This does not necessarily imply an artistic ability; rather a liking of being surrounded by things of beauty. Enjoying the luxuries of life, Librans are often languid, with a tendency to laziness.

Positive traits
Considerate, courteous Librans enjoy communicating and the companionship of their fellows. They are consummate diplomats and avoid friction whenever possible, using tact rather than aggression when confronted. Amiable peace-lovers, Librans will mediate and try to unite those who are quarrelling. Concerned with balance, subjects are fair-minded with a highly developed sense of justice. They are intelligent, clear-thinking, generally truthful, loyal and display a sympathetic attitude to those less fortunate.

Negative traits
Harmony-seeking Libra can become self-pitying and disillusioned by the natural 'disharmony' of life. Searching too for that 'special' relationship, they can gain a reputation for being flirtatious. The Libran concern with 'weighing the balance' often leads to indecision and an inherent dislike of saying 'No' can cause regret. Procrastination, downright laziness and ultra-sensitivity are common faults with Libra – as also is vanity, when a preoccupation with appearance becomes over-stressed.

September

1949 Bruce Springsteen, American rock singer and composer, b. Freehold, New Jersey

23

1896 F. Scott Fitzgerald, American novelist, b. St. Paul, Minnesota

24

1906 Dmitri Shostakovich, Russian composer, b. St. Petersburg

25

1888 T.S. Eliot, British writer and poet, b. St. Louis, Missouri

26

1895 George Raft, American film actor, b. New York City

27

1934 Brigitte Bardot, French film actress, b. Paris

28

1931 Anita Ekberg, Swedish film actress, b. Malmö

29/30

1935 Johnny Mathis, American singer, b. San Francisco, California

Libra, the seventh sign of the Zodiac, rules from 23rd September to 23rd October and it is said that were day and night to be weighed when the Sun is in Libra, both would be equal.

Sense of 'Self'
For realisation of self, Libra requires a balanced relationship with one special 'other'.
Key phrase: 'Together, we will enjoy perfect harmony'.

The Mythology of Libra

Libra represents Balance or the Scales of Justice and typifies equilibrium. In the ancient Egyptian zodiac, however, its glyph shows a sunset over the Earth and represents the 'Male' Sun with the 'Female' Earth beneath, and the 'space of air' between. While first-century Roman astrologer Tarutius maintained that the foundation of Rome in 753 BC took place during the span of Libra, thereby investing Italy with a Libran significance, Leo is now held to represent Rome and Italy. The ancients told that Libra and Scorpio were once a single figure, with Libra envisaged as being held in the claws of Scorpio and known as the 'claws of the Scorpion'.

Ruling planet: Venus
Venus, daughter of Jupiter and Dione, wife of Vulcan and loved by Mars and Anchises was, to the Romans, a nature goddess who brought forth Spring flowers and vines. Mythologically, Venus was also known as the morning star of war and the evening star of harlotry and love. Ruler of Taurus and Libra, Venus (Mistress of Friday), brings harmony and a love of the arts to both signs. In Taurus, this is expressed as a love of beauty and a desire to possess beautiful things. In Libra, Venus grants personal beauty with the desire for harmonious conditions, particularly within special relationships. (See also Taurus section).

October

1935 Julie Andrews, English actress and singer, b. Walton-on-Thames, Surrey

1

1890 'Groucho' Marx, American comedian, b. New York City

2

Greek legend associates Libra with Mochis, inventor of weights and measures. Libra's span also covers the time of weighing the harvest.

1925 Gore Vidal, American writer and critic, b. West Point, New York

3

The ancients believed the Libran to be particularly trustworthy and to be able to handle another person's money with honesty – even if he had none himself.

1895 Buster Keaton, American comedy film actor, b. Piqua, Kansas

4

1830 Chester Arthur, 21st President of the United States, b. Fairfield, Vermont

5

1820 Jenny Lind, Swedish opera singer, b. Stockholm

6

1939 Clive James, Australian author and television presenter, b. Sydney

7

Relationships

Compatible signs: Aquarius and Gemini
Polar (opposite) sign: Aries
*With communicativeness and a keen intellect linking
all three Air signs, charming Libra is agreeably
affectionate with a strong desire to please – albeit
continually 'weighing the balance' with regard to
partners. Should these be found lacking, Libra cools
and continues the search for that significant 'other'.
Cool Aquarius could be a faithful, fair-minded partner,
given space to pursue mental interests and meet friends
at the club. Lively Gemini could override Libra's
natural laziness and bring versatility to a relationship.
Partners should encourage positivity to counteract
Libran 'hesitancy' and indecisiveness.*

Careers

*Not generally ambitious, Librans
feel at ease in professions
involving one-to-one counselling,
such as marriage guidance or
career advisers. They excel
particularly in the judicial,
diplomatic and financial fields.
Enjoying clean, equable
surroundings, Librans are
appropriately placed in the world
of fashion and beauty. Careers in
the arts are also applicable to
Venus-influenced Librans – from
artist, collector and valuer to
musician, dancer or juggler.*

Health

*The kidneys, loins, lumbar
regions and the urinary system
are ruled by Libra and problems
and illnesses concerning these
areas prevail. Diseases such as
nephritis, lumbago and urinary
tract infections tend to afflict the
Libran – as do polar sign Aries-
linked headaches. Given Libra's
well-balanced tenor of life,
health is generally good. Care
should be taken to preserve this
equilibrium, and not to allow the
inherent Libran languor to
jeopardise the regime.*

October

1937 Dame Merle Park, Rhodesian ballerina and ballet administrator, b. Salisbury	*8*
1835 Camille Saint-Saëns, French composer and pianist, b. Paris	*9*
1813 Giuseppe Verdi, Italian opera composer, b. Le Rancole, nr. Busseto	*10*
1884 Eleanor Roosevelt, wife of Franklin D. Roosevelt, b. New York City	*11*
1935 Luciano Pavarotti, Italian opera singer, b. Modena	*12*
1853 Lillie Langtry, English actress, b. Jersey, Channel Islands	*13*
1928 Roger Moore, English film actor, b. Stockwell, London	*14*

Traditional associations of Libra
Gemstone: Opal
Metal: Copper
Colours: Lemon yellow, pale blue, pale green and pink
Animals: Lizards and other small reptiles
Cities: Copenhagen, Vienna, Frankfurt and Nottingham
Countries: Austria, Burma, Argentina and Tibet

Lucky for Librans
Day: Friday
Number: Six

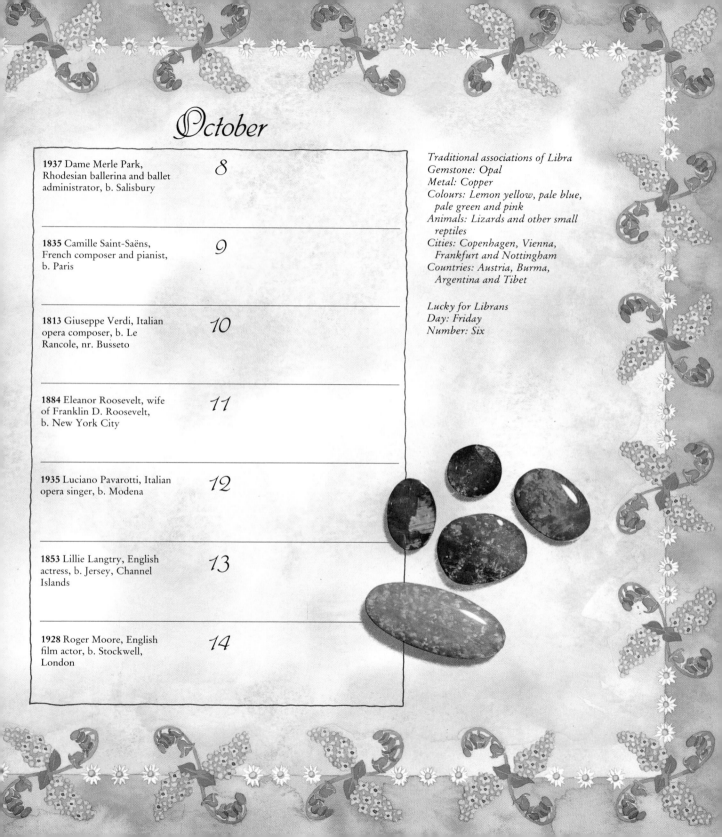

October

Gemstone: Opal

The opal was said to be named from the Sanskrit upala or 'precious stone'. Deriving also from the Greek ops, meaning 'eye' it was considered unlucky to introduce the opal or eye-stone into a house because it interfered with the sanctity of domestic privacy. Thought to be capable of opening the 'third eye', the opal was used by mystics seeking to enter 'supernatural realms'. Showing a variety of colours and patterns, the opal changes both colour and character with prevailing light and temperature, and is said to protect areas of the body which emit and are sources of heat.

Known as the Stone of Hope and Justice, the opal was feared by tyrannical monarchs of old. Though not of this ilk, Queen Elizabeth I declined to wear the gemstone even though she had a considerable collection.

Other monarchs too had reservations about the opal. Reigning Emperors of Russia attributed the Evil Eye to the gemstone and Queen Victoria, though prepared to give them to her daughters on their wedding days, seldom wore one herself.

1880 Marie Stopes, Scottish scientist and pioneer of birth control, b. Edinburgh

15

1854 Oscar Wilde, Irish dramatist and wit, b. Dublin

16

1918 Rita Hayworth, American film actress, b. New York City

17

1956 Martina Navratilova, American tennis player, b. Prague, Czechoslovakia

18

1859 Alfred Dreyfus, French subject of the 'Dreyfus Treason Affair', b. Alsace

19

1904 Anna Neagle, English actress, b. London

20

1917 Dizzy Gillespie, American jazz trumpeter, b. Cheraw, North Carolina

21

October

1811 Franz Liszt, Hungarian composer and pianist, b. Raiding, nr. Oedenburg

22

1931 Diana Dors, English film actress, b. Swindon, Wiltshire

23

Flowers and trees

Flowers
Dahlia: Instability
Daisy: Innocence
Lilac (purple): First emotions of love
Cabbage rose: Ambassador of love
Bluebell: Constancy
Trees
Ash: Grandeur
Poplar (black): Courage
Poplar (white): Time
Others
Berry fruits, apples, pears, grapes. Wheat, barley and other cereals, artichokes, asparagus and almost all spices.

Scorpio

24th October – 22nd November

A Feminine • Negative • Fixed • Water sign

Scorpio, the eighth sign of the Zodiac, is the first one to be aware of the 'mysticism' beyond physical reality. Associated with deep, powerful passions and having a rare personal magnetism, Water sign Scorpio is intuitive, secretive and cautious. Concerned with probing 'hidden depths', the investigative professions are often appropriate for Scorpios.

Planetary Influence

Anciently attributed to Mars, Scorpio is more recently and appropriately associated with Pluto. Both planets imply aggression – in Mars outgoing, fiery and energetic, and in Pluto explosive, intense and with passionate, powerful associations. Scorpio is all of these things, but less overtly so than in Mars, expressing a deviousness and the secretiveness of its Water element. The Plutonian violence, symbolised by the death (elimination) and the renewal or regenerative process, is more truly Scorpionic, giving emotional energy and being expressed in the desire to bring to the surface that which is hidden, to eradicate and to emerge, renewed and enlightened by this transformation.

Positive traits
Scorpios are intensely passionate and devoted to that which is theirs – be it partner, family, career or 'cause'. They are reliable, cautious, often restrained in manner and prove to be 'safe' confidantes who keep secrets and true feelings well hidden. Highly analytical, resourceful, accepting and adapting easily to change, Scorpios often solve problems intuitively. Imaginative and with a compelling personal magnetism, this sign possesses a strong sense of purpose and never does things by halves.

Negative traits
It is often said, with some truth, that – in terms of its negative characteristics – Scorpio is the 'worst sign in the Zodiac'. Its natural caution, if over-stressed, can lead to jealousy and suspicion of those around and havoc may be caused by the sign's misdirected passions, fertile imagination, an inherent ruthlessness, and biting 'sting-in-the-tail' remarks which can be both hurtful and damaging to the recipient. A slighted Scorpion is uncompromising in its bitterness with hatred and enmity often lasting a lifetime.

October

1882 Dame Sybil Thorndike, English stage and film actress, b. Gainsborough, Lincolnshire

24

1881 Pablo Picasso, Spanish artist, b. Malaga, Andalusia

25

1879 Leon Trotsky, Russian revolutionary leader, b. Yanovka, Ukraine

26 GEORGINA

1914 Dylan Thomas, Welsh poet, b. Swansea

27

1927 Cleo Laine, English singer, b. London

28

Honeysuckle brought into a house foretold of a wedding and its presence in a young girl's bedroom was thought to encourage erotic dreams ... Honeysuckle is attributed to Scorpio.

1740 James Boswell, Scottish biographer and diarist, b. Edinburgh

29

'... The fairest flowers o' the season Are our carnations and the streak'd gillyvors'
William Shakespeare, The Winter's Tale, *Act iv, Sc. 4*

1751 Richard Brinsley Sheridan, Irish dramatist, b. Dublin

30/31

1632 Jan Vermeer, Dutch artist, b. Delft

The Mythology of Scorpio

The ancients followed Virgo with Scorpio in their Zodiacs. Both signs are analytical by nature – in the 'material' and 'emotional' senses respectively. Later, Libra was placed between, the Scales being held in the claws of Scorpio. Indicating Scorpio's power to destroy or preserve the life-forces, its image can portray either the 'degenerate', earthbound Scorpio or the 'regenerated' Scorpio, seen as the heavenly-aspiring Eagle. The Scorpio glyph, similar to that of Virgo, represents the Creation myth of Man and Woman – and their Fall, symbolised by the Serpent's sting or tail. The barbed end of the glyph could also indicate Scorpio's 'stinging' tongue!

Ruling planet: Pluto

Pluto, unseen ruler of the dead and guardian of the Underworld, is known in Greek mythology as Hades. Influencing eruptions, major upheavals, earthquakes, volcanoes and explosions, Pluto symbolises beginnings and endings; death and life beyond death. It is a force for both creation and destruction. Its glyph combines the initials of astronomer Percival Lowell, who predicted the planet's existence in 1916 but who did not live to witness its actual discovery on 18th February 1930.

Ancient ruling planet: Mars

Mars, God of War and the second most important deity in the Roman pantheon, was eclipsed only by Jupiter. He was the father of Romulus and Remus, his sister-wife was Bellona and Venus was his mistress. Signifying brutality, aggression and wrath, the outgoing energy of Mars, hotly and incisively expressed, is no longer held to typify the turbulent depths of Scorpio's intense, passionate nature. Instead, Pluto is now felt more accurately to typify the Scorpio character. (See also Aries section).

November

1887 L.S. Lowry, English artist, b. Manchester

1   RUBINA

1755 Marie Antoinette, Austrian princess, b. Vienna

2

1949 Larry Holmes, American heavyweight boxing champion, b. Cuthbert, Georgia

3

1918 Art Carney, American film actor, b. Mount Vernon, New York

4

1913 Vivien Leigh, English actress, b. Darjeeling, India

5

1892 Sir John Alcock, English aviator, b. Manchester

6

1867 Marie Curie, Polish-French scientist, b. Warsaw

7

In Greek mythology, Hera is said to have sent the Scorpion to sting the hunter Orion as a punishment for his vanity in boasting that he could kill any animal, large or small. Zeus then placed the Scorpion in the Heavens, whereupon it was called Scorpius – the constellational image of the Zodiac sign of Scorpio.

Relationships

Compatible signs: *Cancer and Pisces*
Polar (opposite) sign: *Taurus*
To Scorpio, 'love' is all-consuming. Sexual love represents the challenge of transcending the physical to reach a rare emotion of mystical intensity. Fellow Water signs Cancer and Pisces identify with the lure of the mystically 'religious' experience, and receptive Cancer would warm to Scorpio's dependability and passionate devotion to family. Pisces, irresistibly drawn to Scorpio, could discover that though compatible, their combined intuitiveness is a mixed blessing. A tendency to indulge their passions too generously, to use their 'animal' magnetism too cunningly, makes the Scorpion a volatile, often disruptive partner.

Careers
Work involving analytical processes, as with the scientist, researcher and criminal investigator, allows Scorpio to express its practical aspects. The secretive aspect of Scorpio is seen in the work of the psychoanalyst and a mediumistic gift for healing would be aptly expressed by a doctor or spiritual healer. Careers connected with the sea are applicable to Water sign Scorpio, as also are those with the 'cutting' Mars influence, such as surgeon, butcher or hairdresser.

Health
Representing the secret mysteries of the life-force itself, Scorpio has rule over the generative organs and, symbolising the 'elimination' process prior to renewal, the anus. Ailments tend to be located in the genitals, prostate gland, bladder and colon. A link with Taurus brings vulnerability to the throat. Ruptures and abscesses may also occur. Female Scorpios can suffer uterine and womb problems. Mental rest is advised to maintain positive health.

November

1847 Bram Stoker, Irish novelist, b. Dublin	*8*
1909 Katherine Hepburn, American film actress, b. Hartford, Connecticut	*9*
1697 William Hogarth, English painter and engraver, b. London	*10*
1821 Fyodor Dostoyevsky, Russian author, b. Moscow	*11*
1840 Auguste Rodin, French sculptor, b. Paris	*12*
1850 Robert Louis Stevenson, Scottish author, b. Edinburgh	*13*
1919 Veronica Lake, American film actress, b. Lake Placid, New York	*14*

Sense of 'Self'
To Scorpio, living is a series of 'deaths and resurrections'. Through the process of elimination and renewal, Scorpio seeks the fulfilment of regeneration.
Key phrase: 'I experience all things with intensity, passion – and purpose'.

November

Gemstones: Topaz and malachite

A form of beryl, the topaz occurs in several colours but the rich gold variety symbolises the Sun in the mineral kingdom, typifies courage and leadership and is said to make its wearer fearless and wise. Giving power over wild beasts, the topaz implies the conquest of Scorpio's baser nature and transcendence to nobler realms. Malachite is one of the group of silicates and is formed from oxidised materials on copper ores. It is recognised by its swirling patterns of rich green banding and may be said to symbolise the 'swirling' turbulent depths of the Scorpio nature.

Legend tells how the topaz was discovered by shipwrecked mariners awaiting rescue on a small fog-enshrouded island. Though difficult to locate, they were found and subsequently named both island and gemstone Topazos – meaning: 'lost and found'.

Malachite is said to invest the wearer with the power of understanding the speech of animals, increase resistance to disease and banish melancholy. It is also thought to help those with bone calcification – sustaining sufferers on a 'spiritual' level.

1738 Sir William Herschel, English astronomer, b. Hanover, Germany

15

1896 Sir Oswald Mosley, British politician, b. London

16

1887 Field Marshal Viscount Montgomery, British World War II army commander, b. London

17

1836 Sir W.S. Gilbert, playwright and librettist, b. London

18

1917 Indira Gandhi, Indian stateswoman and Prime Minister, b. Allahabad

19

1889 Edwin Hubble, American astronomer, b. Marshfield, Missouri

20

1945 Goldie Hawn, American film actress, b. Washington D.C.

21

November

1819 George Eliot, English novelist, b. Nuneaton, Warwickshire

22

Flowers and trees

Flowers
Red chrysanthemum: I love
Red carnation: Alas! for my poor heart
Rhododendron: Danger or Beware
Honeysuckle: Generous and devoted affection
Gentian: Transcendence
Trees
Blackthorn: Difficulty
Thorn apple: Deceitful charms
Hawthorn: Hope
Branch of thorn: Severity
Others
Strong tasting foods, onions, hops, leeks and shallots. Most of the pungent, sharp tasting foods attributable to Mars and Aries.

Traditional associations of Scorpio
Gemstones: Topaz and malachite
Metal: Plutonium
Colours: Dark red, maroon and smoky cloud formations
Animals: Snakes, insects and other invertebrates
Cities: New Orleans, Cincinnati, Valencia and Liverpool
Countries: Morocco, Norway, Uruguay and Syria

Lucky for Scorpios
Day: Tuesday
Number: Nine

Sagittarius

23rd November – 21st December

A Masculine • Positive • Mutable • Fire sign

Ninth sign of the Zodiac, Sagittarius is the most advanced of the Fire signs, recognising and expressing its will within society and developing wide-ranging intellectual interests to a more profound degree. Valuing personal freedom and self-expression, expansive, outgoing Sagittarians are optimistic, outspoken and enjoy travel and sporting activities.

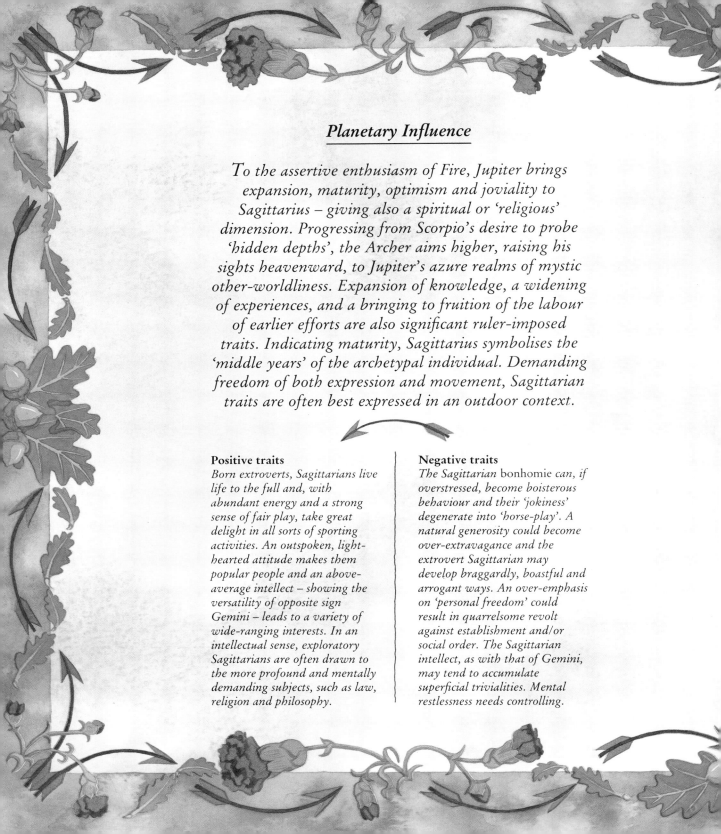

Planetary Influence

To the assertive enthusiasm of Fire, Jupiter brings expansion, maturity, optimism and joviality to Sagittarius – giving also a spiritual or 'religious' dimension. Progressing from Scorpio's desire to probe 'hidden depths', the Archer aims higher, raising his sights heavenward, to Jupiter's azure realms of mystic other-worldliness. Expansion of knowledge, a widening of experiences, and a bringing to fruition of the labour of earlier efforts are also significant ruler-imposed traits. Indicating maturity, Sagittarius symbolises the 'middle years' of the archetypal individual. Demanding freedom of both expression and movement, Sagittarian traits are often best expressed in an outdoor context.

Positive traits

Born extroverts, Sagittarians live life to the full and, with abundant energy and a strong sense of fair play, take great delight in all sorts of sporting activities. An outspoken, light-hearted attitude makes them popular people and an above-average intellect – showing the versatility of opposite sign Gemini – leads to a variety of wide-ranging interests. In an intellectual sense, exploratory Sagittarians are often drawn to the more profound and mentally demanding subjects, such as law, religion and philosophy.

Negative traits

The Sagittarian bonhomie *can, if overstressed, become boisterous behaviour and their 'jokiness' degenerate into 'horse-play'. A natural generosity could become over-extravagance and the extrovert Sagittarian may develop braggardly, boastful and arrogant ways. An over-emphasis on 'personal freedom' could result in quarrelsome revolt against establishment and/or social order. The Sagittarian intellect, as with that of Gemini, may tend to accumulate superficial trivialities. Mental restlessness needs controlling.*

November

1887 Boris Karloff, English film actor, b. Dulwich, London

23

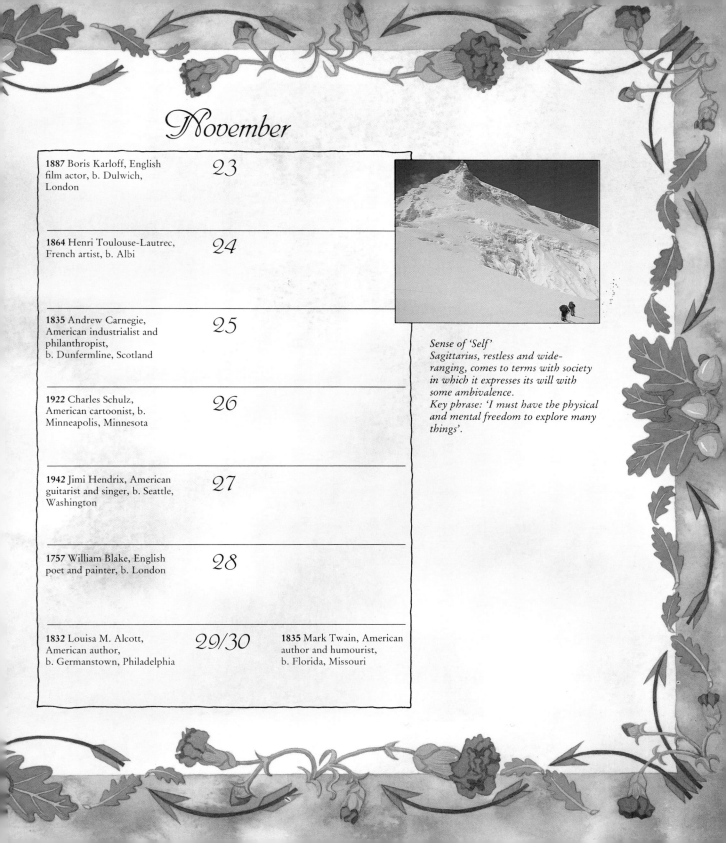

1864 Henri Toulouse-Lautrec, French artist, b. Albi

24

1835 Andrew Carnegie, American industrialist and philanthropist, b. Dunfermline, Scotland

25

Sense of 'Self'
Sagittarius, restless and wide-ranging, comes to terms with society in which it expresses its will with some ambivalence.
Key phrase: 'I must have the physical and mental freedom to explore many things'.

1922 Charles Schulz, American cartoonist, b. Minneapolis, Minnesota

26

1942 Jimi Hendrix, American guitarist and singer, b. Seattle, Washington

27

1757 William Blake, English poet and painter, b. London

28

1832 Louisa M. Alcott, American author, b. Germanstown, Philadelphia

29/30

1835 Mark Twain, American author and humourist, b. Florida, Missouri

The Mythology of Sagittarius

This figure is most often represented as a Centaur or Satyr – half-man and half-beast – with drawn bow, later simplified into a three-headed arrow which was said to represent spiritual aspiration, aiming heavenward to spiritual realms. The Sagittarian myth concerns Chiron who, in Greek mythology, was known as the wise centaur, a healer, sage and teacher. He was also an excellent hunter and sportsman who, at death, was transformed by Jupiter into a constellation of stars. Sagittarius is associated also with a demonic archer named Sagittary, half-man, half-beast, whose eyes sparkled like fire and who struck down opponents in battle like lightning. As Shakespeare wrote in Troilus and Cressida, 'the dreadful Sagittary appals our numbers'.

Ruling planet: Jupiter

Jupiter, the all-powerful, ruled from his kingdom in the Heavens. He was the Prince of Light, his colour was azure and his metal was tin. He made known the future through the flight of birds and other signs in the Heavens. Early astrologers designated him the shepherd of the stars and giver of abundance.

Acknowledged by the Romans as their patron and lord, Jupiter Optimus Maximus, many festivals were celebrated in his honour. Signifying success of every kind, the most benign, the most dignified of the Gods has been worshipped under various names in many lands and cultures of the world. (See also Pisces section).

December

1910 Dame Alicia Markova, English prima ballerina, b. London

1

1899 Sir John Barbirolli, English conductor and musical director, b. London

2

1923 Maria Callas, Greek operatic soprano, b. New York City

3

1865 Edith Cavell, English nurse and patriot, b. Swardeston, Norfolk

4

1901 Walt Disney, American cartoon film producer, b. Chicago, Illinois

5

1920 Dave Brubeck, American jazz pianist and composer, b. California

6

1863 Pietro Mascagni, Italian composer, b. Livorno

7

In Greek mythology, Chiron was the wise centaur. In astrology, this is the sign of the wounded healer bringing benefits to others which have been discovered during the process of healing.

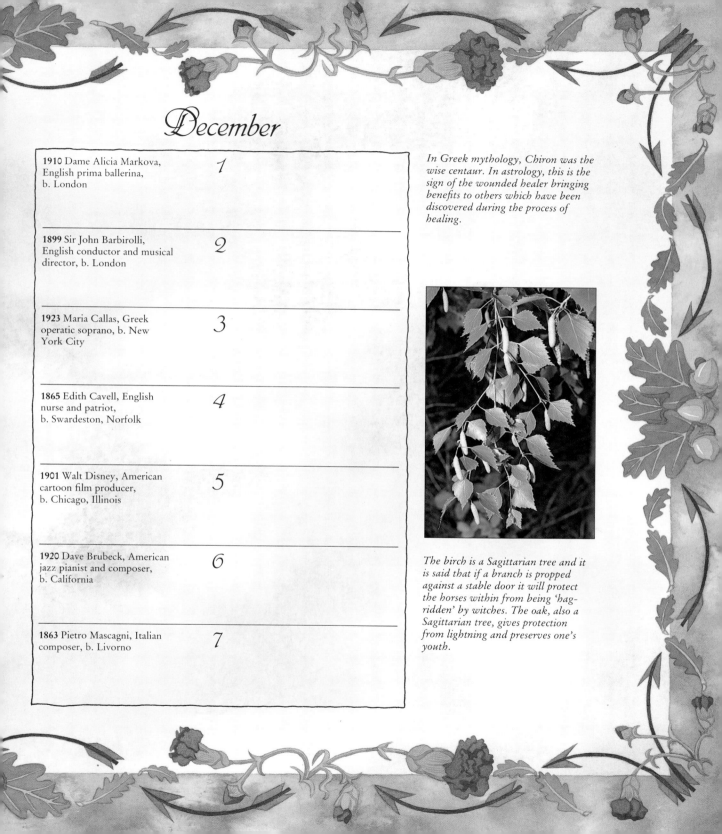

The birch is a Sagittarian tree and it is said that if a branch is propped against a stable door it will protect the horses within from being 'hag-ridden' by witches. The oak, also a Sagittarian tree, gives protection from lightning and preserves one's youth.

Relationships

Compatible signs: Aries and Leo
Polar (opposite) sign: Gemini
Fire sign Sagittarius is ardent but often difficult to understand with mutable feelings that quickly change. The Archer's need for personal freedom may mean that relationships are cast aside because of this. Fiery Aries has strong sexual feelings and would also bring mental stimulation to a relationship. Both signs enjoy the excitement of intellectual and verbal challenge – even if this does cause a 'flaming' row! Rampant Leo is passionate but sincerely affectionate too, and Sagittarius will appreciate the Lion's benign guidance when 'happy go lucky' plans fall through.

Careers

Suitable careers should allow both the physical and mental aspects of Sagittarius to be given equal freedom for development. Sporting and outdoor professions are applicable, such as in the competitive, exploratory and (particularly) the hunting 'fields'. Given the symbolic Sagittarian link with the horse, all work connected with these animals is ideal. The intellectual professions also appeal, such as writer, lawyer, teacher and priest and philosopher. Sagittarians are also appropriately employed as translators of foreign languages.

Health

Sagittarius has rule over the thighs, hips and liver. Sciatica and hip joint problems are prevalent and rheumatism and rheumatic fever are common ailments. Jupiterian over-indulgence may cause dysfunction of the liver and the Sagittarian preoccupation with sport and physical activity can often result in accidents. Psychological upset, mental strain or nervous exhaustion following intense restlessness, as in opposite sign Gemini, will need to be offset by periods of relaxation – perhaps of a meditative nature.

December

1894 James Thurber, American humourist and artist, b. Columbus, Ohio

8

1915 Elizabeth Schwarzkopf, German opera singer, b. Jarotschin, Posen

9

1891 Earl Alexander of Tunis, British Army Commander in World War II, b. Caledon, County Tyrone

10

1913 Carlo Ponti, Italian film director, b. Milan

11

1915 Frank Sinatra, American singer and entertainer, b. Hoboken, New Jersey

12

1936 HH Prince Karim, Aga Khan IV, b. Geneva, Switzerland

13

1895 King George VI, father of Queen Elizabeth II of England, b. Sandringham, Norfolk

14

Traditional associations of Sagittarius
Gemstone: Turquoise
Metal: Tin
Colours: Rich purple, violet, red and indigo
Animals: Those which are hunted – deer etc.
Cities: Toledo, Budapest, Sheffield and Toronto
Countries: Spain, Australia, South Africa and Arabia

Lucky for Sagittarians
Day: Thursday
Number: Three

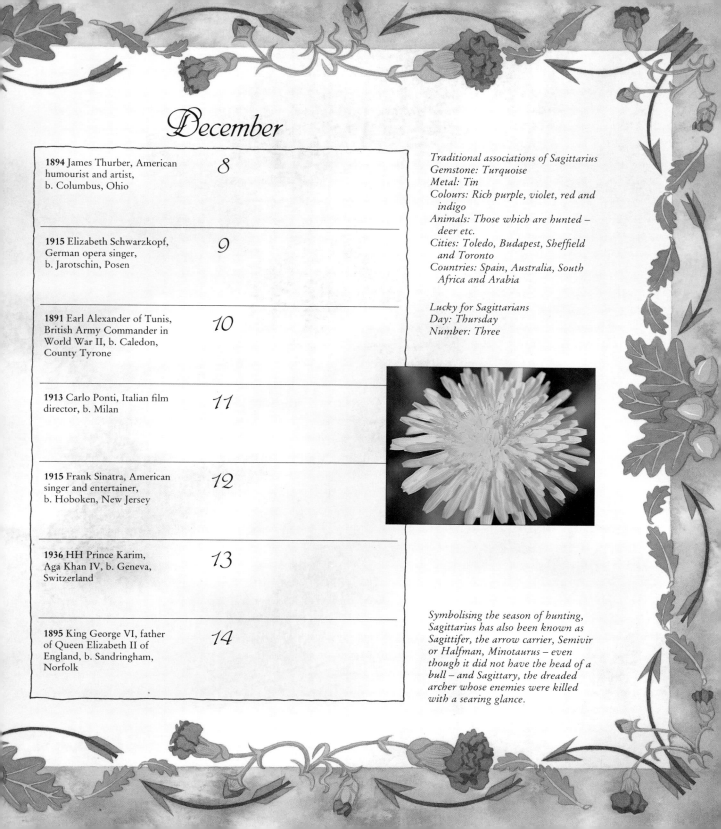

Symbolising the season of hunting, Sagittarius has also been known as Sagittifer, the arrow carrier, Semivir or Halfman, Minotaurus – even though it did not have the head of a bull – and Sagittary, the dreaded archer whose enemies were killed with a searing glance.

Gemstone: Turquoise

The turquoise is a basic aluminium phosphate with a small amount of copper giving it its distinctive blue-green colour. Originally from Turkey, turquoise has been a much sought-after gem; in the Aztec civilisation it held precedence over gold. Symbolising beauty to the Egyptians, many fine pieces of jewellery were made from the gemstone, and from strips of turquoise the lotus flower was replicated. Considered to be a royal jewel and treasured by the Kings of Persia, turquoise was thought to protect horses and their riders and to be a safeguard against the Evil Eye.

It is said that if a person feels at ease with turquoise, it will serve that person well. In gemstone healing, the turquoise, ideally set in silver, is thought to 'harmonise' the spiritual self.

With the emerald, the turquoise has been used in ancient rituals to incite love and passion and ensure mutual fidelity. To dream of the gemstone is said to herald a new and long-lasting friendship.

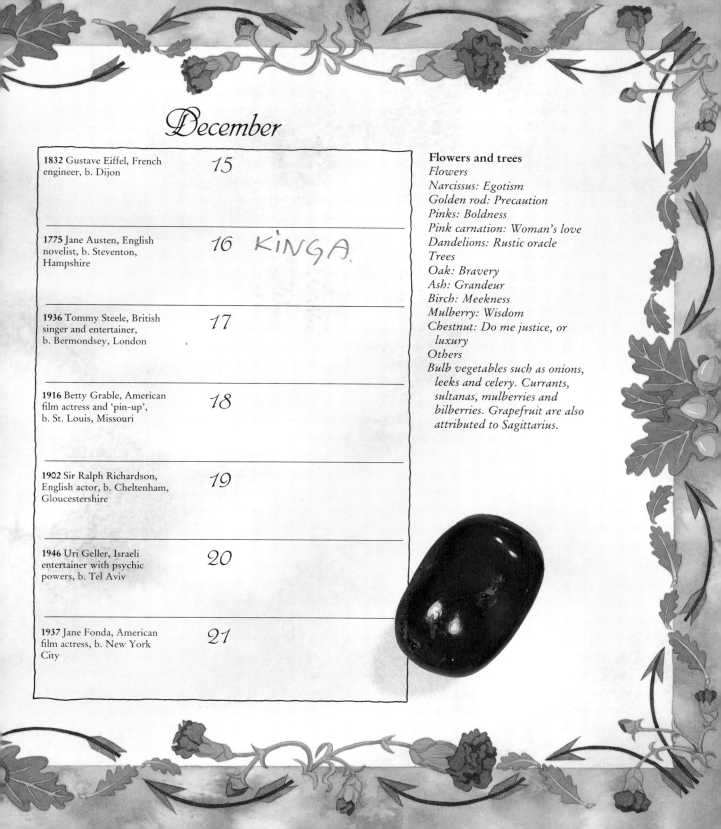

December

1832 Gustave Eiffel, French engineer, b. Dijon	*15*	
1775 Jane Austen, English novelist, b. Steventon, Hampshire	*16*	KINGA.
1936 Tommy Steele, British singer and entertainer, b. Bermondsey, London	*17*	
1916 Betty Grable, American film actress and 'pin-up', b. St. Louis, Missouri	*18*	
1902 Sir Ralph Richardson, English actor, b. Cheltenham, Gloucestershire	*19*	
1946 Uri Geller, Israeli entertainer with psychic powers, b. Tel Aviv	*20*	
1937 Jane Fonda, American film actress, b. New York City	*21*	

Flowers and trees

Flowers
Narcissus: Egotism
Golden rod: Precaution
Pinks: Boldness
Pink carnation: Woman's love
Dandelions: Rustic oracle
Trees
Oak: Bravery
Ash: Grandeur
Birch: Meekness
Mulberry: Wisdom
Chestnut: Do me justice, or
  luxury
Others
Bulb vegetables such as onions,
  leeks and celery. Currants,
  sultanas, mulberries and
  bilberries. Grapefruit are also
  attributed to Sagittarius.

Capricorn

22nd December – 20th January

A Feminine • Negative • Cardinal • Earth sign

Tenth sign of the Zodiac, Capricorn symbolises old age and the father-figure relating to, and the embodiment of, authority. Practical, prudent, cautious and controlled, the aspiring Goat climbs slowly yet resolutely to the top of the mountain. This is the sign of politicians and administrators, power and officialdom.

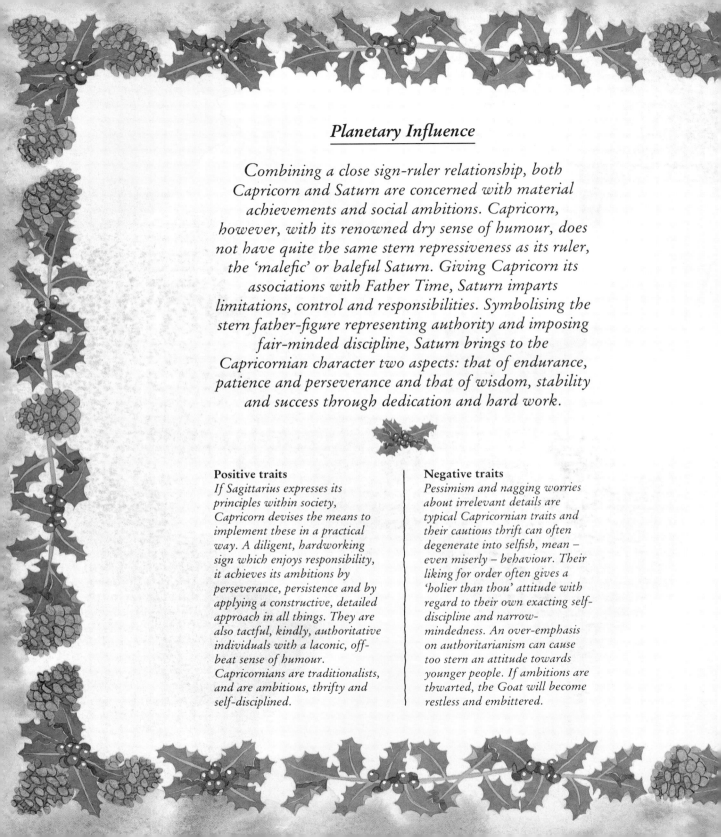

Planetary Influence

Combining a close sign-ruler relationship, both Capricorn and Saturn are concerned with material achievements and social ambitions. Capricorn, however, with its renowned dry sense of humour, does not have quite the same stern repressiveness as its ruler, the 'malefic' or baleful Saturn. Giving Capricorn its associations with Father Time, Saturn imparts limitations, control and responsibilities. Symbolising the stern father-figure representing authority and imposing fair-minded discipline, Saturn brings to the Capricornian character two aspects: that of endurance, patience and perseverance and that of wisdom, stability and success through dedication and hard work.

Positive traits

If Sagittarius expresses its principles within society, Capricorn devises the means to implement these in a practical way. A diligent, hardworking sign which enjoys responsibility, it achieves its ambitions by perseverance, persistence and by applying a constructive, detailed approach in all things. They are also tactful, kindly, authoritative individuals with a laconic, off-beat sense of humour. Capricornians are traditionalists, and are ambitious, thrifty and self-disciplined.

Negative traits

Pessimism and nagging worries about irrelevant details are typical Capricornian traits and their cautious thrift can often degenerate into selfish, mean – even miserly – behaviour. Their liking for order often gives a 'holier than thou' attitude with regard to their own exacting self-discipline and narrow-mindedness. An over-emphasis on authoritarianism can cause too stern an attitude towards younger people. If ambitions are thwarted, the Goat will become restless and embittered.

December

1858 Giacomo Puccini, Italian opera composer, b. Lucca	*22*
1888 J. Arthur Rank, British film magnate, b. Hull, Humberside	*23*
1922 Ava Gardner, American film actress, b. Smithfield, North Carolina	*24*
1642 Sir Isaac Newton, English mathematician and scientist, b. nr. Grantham	*25*
1893 Mao Tse-Tung, Chinese revolutionary and statesman, b. Shaoshan, Hunan	*26*
1901 Marlene Dietrich, German film actress, b. Berlin	*27*
1934 Dame Maggie Smith, English actress, b. Ilford, Essex	*28*

Sense of 'Self'
With persistence and perseverance, the Goat climbs ever upward to reach the heights of material success. Key phrase: 'I did it!'

The Capricorn glyph is said to symbolise the duality of conscious versus subconscious forces. This is represented by the Goat's horn and vestigial fish tail and is described as the sign's materialistic 'conscious' predominating over the 'mysticism' of the subconscious.

The Mythology of Capricorn

Capricorn is seen in many guises – as the fish-tailed Babylonian god Ea, who rose from the deep to teach wisdom to Man; and as the Greek god Pan who, fearful of Typhon, changed himself into a goat and jumped into the Nile. Emerging as half-goat, half-fish, Zeus placed him in the heavens as Capricorn. Seen also as a winged goat or dragon, drawing the chariot of Saturn, it was said that Time ended with Capricorn – also known as the Gate of Death. Opposite sign Cancer symbolises the Gate of Birth. Occultist Madame Blavatsky claimed Capricorn as the 'most sacred and mysterious' of the signs.

Ruling planet: Saturn
Saturn, ruler of Capricorn and Lord of Saturday – known also as Chronos (Time) – is said to have devoured all his children except Jupiter, Neptune and Pluto. Metaphorically, Jupiter was air, Neptune, water and Pluto, the grave. These, it is said, Time cannot consume. . . Honouring Saturn, the Romans celebrated 'Saturnalia' on the 17th, 18th and 19th December – *a festival later extended to seven days. A time of licensed disorder and misrule reigned when masters served slaves and kings were chosen from criminals and vagabonds. Saturn's glyph represents the semi-circle of Soul with the Cross of Matter predominantly placed to indicate life's material elements. (See also Aquarius section).*

December

1721 Madame de Pompadour, French mistress of King Louis XV, b. Paris

29

1865 Rudyard Kipling, English poet and author, b. Bombay, India

30

1869 Henri Matisse, French artist, b. Le Cateau

31

Traditional associations of Capricorn
Gemstone: Garnet
Metal: Lead
Colours: Dark grey, black, dark
*   brown and indigo*
Animals: Goats and other cloven-
*   footed creatures*
Cities: Delhi, Mexico City, Ghent
*   and Brussels*
Countries: India, Mexico, Macedonia
*   and Orkney and Shetland*

Lucky for Capricornians
Day: Saturday
Number: Eight

'*Make use of Time, let not advantage*
*   slip*'
William Shakespeare, Venus and
Adonis

Relationships

Compatible signs: Taurus and Virgo
Polar (opposite) sign: Cancer
Cautious Capricorns are responsible – sometimes reproving – parents and partners, but their prudent handling of practical matters provides a solid and stable background. Patient Taurus and careful Capricorn, both unashamedly earth-bound with money (security) on their minds, albeit warmth and humour in their respective souls, could be a winning combination – Venus bringing a sultry sensuality to Saturn's wintry ways. Industrious Virgo will approve of practical Capricorn and together they could make a respectable couple. Passions may be slow moving but will be rewardingly earth-shattering!

Careers

Caves, mining and all underground work are traditionally associated with Capricorn. However, given their orderliness and organisational skills, any business requiring these abilities is appropriate: Capricorn will carry out orders from above and ensure that those below do their duty. This would also apply to those Capricornians who enter the Church, armed forces or teaching fields. Building and construction work is suitable.

Health

Limiting diseases of rheumatoid/ arthritic origin are common Capricornian complaints as both Saturn and Capricorn rule the skeletal system – especially the knees. The skin may also be potentially troublesome. Eczema and psoriasis prevail, both known to be stress-related and the last a rheumatoid-related condition. Diseases associated with cold and old age (such as osteoporosis) are common, as are digestive problems due to stress.

January

1879 William Fox, American film magnate, b. Hungary

1

1920 Isaac Asimov, American biochemist and science fiction author, b. Petrovichi, USSR

2

1892 J.R.R. Tolkien, English academic and author, b. Bloemfontein, South Africa

3

1878 Augustus John, English portrait painter, b. Tenby, Wales

4

1876 Konrad Adenauer, German statesman and Chancellor, b. Cologne

5

1412 St. Joan of Arc, French patriot and martyr, b. Domrémy

6

1925 Gerald Durrell, British zoologist and writer, b. Jamshedpur, India

7

'There's rosemary, that's for remembrance. Pray, love, remember. And there is pansies; that's for thoughts.'
William Shakespeare, Hamlet, *Act iv*, Sc. 5

January

Gemstone: Garnet

Treasured throughout the ages and particularly admired by the Victorians, the garnet, in which the Romans saw a resemblance to the fleshy pips of the pomegranate, is one of the silicate group. It is seen in three varieties: pyrope (yellow or crimson), almandine (brown-red) and spessartine (orange-red to near black). Holistically, the garnet is said to be most effective in curing depression and in strengthening a patient's will to be cured. Significantly, as the gemstone attributed to Capricorn, it is also held to be beneficial in the treatment of arthritis and other calcification complaints to which the sign is prone.

The garnet may be faceted, carved or rounded and polished into a dome. This last is called a 'cabochon' from the French word caboche *meaning 'head'. To the garnet cabochon, which was popularly featured in jewellery of that time, the Victorians gave the name 'carbuncle'.*

Thought by some also to be appropriate to Capricorn is chalcedony, a gemstone closely related to agate, and said to drive away melancholy and protect from the depressing influences of Saturn, the ruling planet of Capricorn.

1935 Elvis Presley, American singer, b. Tupelo, Mississippi — **8**

1941 Joan Baez, American folk singer, b. Staten Island, New York — **9**

1903 Dame Barbara Hepworth, English sculptress, b. Wakefield, Yorkshire — **10**

1807 Ezra Cornell, American philanthropist, b. Westchester Landing, New York — **11**

1628 Charles Perrault, French writer and collector of fairy tales, b. Paris — **12** CLAUDE

1884 Sophie Tucker, American singer, b. Russia — **13**

1904 Cecil Beaton, English photographer and theatrical designer, b. London — **14**

January

1906 Aristotle Onassis, Greek shipowner, b. Smyrna, Turkey	*15*
1909 Ethel Merman, American singer, b. Astoria, New York	*16*
1860 Anton Chekhov, Russian dramatist and writer, b. Taganrog	*17*
1904 Cary Grant, American film actor, b. Bristol, England	*18*
1839 Paul Cézanne, French artist, b. Aix-en-Provence	*19*
1920 Federico Fellini, Italian film director, b. Rimini	*20*

Flowers and trees

Flowers
Red poppy: Consolation
Amaranthus: Immortality or
*   unfading love*
Pansy: Thoughts
Red carnation: Alas! for my poor
*   heart*
Trees
Elm: Dignity
Pine: Hope in adversity
Aspen: Lamentation
Poplar: Courage
Holly: Foresight
Weeping willow: Mourning
Others
Potatoes, beets, barley and malt
*   are attributed to Capricorn –*
*   also starchy foods, onions,*
*   spinach and quinces.*

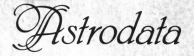

Astrodata

The Quadruplicities or Qualities

Cardinal: Active, outgoing and energetic, Cardinal signs are initiatory and pioneering. If natural assertiveness is thwarted, they become restless, unstable, ultra-sensitive and over-excitable.

Fixed: Cautious, reliable, practical, stubborn, showing tenacity of purpose and disliking change. If over-stressed, Fixed signs can become over-indulgent, lazy, unscrupulous and inconsistent.

Mutable: Adaptable, versatile, flexible, changeable – all Mutable traits indicating the mental processes. If over-stressed, subjects can be selfish and unstable with an inability to make decisions.

The Triplicities or Elements

Each of the following four categories contain three Sun signs:

Fire: Enthusiastic and energetic – Aries, Leo, Sagittarius

Earth: Cautious and practical – Taurus, Virgo, Capricorn

Air: Communicative and intellectual – Gemini, Libra, Aquarius

Water: Emotional and impressionable – Cancer, Scorpio, Pisces

Masculine/Positive and Feminine/Negative

Masculine or Positive: Self-expressive. Extroverted
Feminine or Negative: Self-repressive. Introverted

Masculine/Positive signs express an outgoing, assertive, creative nature: an *outpouring* of self-expression.
Feminine/Negative signs imply receptiveness, intuitiveness and an introspective nature: a *contemplative* self-repression.

The Lights*, Planets and their Keywords

☉	Sun:	Power. Vitality
☽	Moon:	Responses. Fluctuation
☿	Mercury:	Communications. Mentality
♀	Venus:	Harmony. Relationships
♂	Mars:	Energy. Drive
♃	Jupiter:	Expansion. Maturity
♄	Saturn:	Limitation. Control
♅	Uranus:	Change. Disruption
♆	Neptune:	Intuition. Nebulousness
♇	Pluto:	Elimination. Regeneration

*The Sun and the Moon are known as the Greater and Lesser Lights, respectively.

Polar or Opposite Signs

The North and South Poles are excellent examples of 'polarity'. Each are diametrically opposed and both have a common link: severe weather conditions. The same principle applies to the Zodiacal circle:

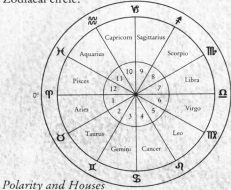

Polarity and Houses

Polar or *opposite* Sun signs also have common links. The association is seen, for instance, in health matters. Arian headaches may be a result of kidney problems – the area of the body ruled by Libra. As Pisces rules the feet, so Virgo rules the hands. Polar signs may also enjoy personal relationships which are enriched with a special empathy and understanding.

The term *opposite* in the above context does not imply 'opposition' in either a conversational or an astrological sense. Astrologically, two planets in 'opposition' are 180° apart in a birth chart – the second most important astrological aspect.

The Twelve Houses

The first six relate directly to the person, defining characteristics and motivations. The final six Houses deal with the subject's immediate environment and their relationships within society. An integral part of preparing a Birth Chart, the following interpretations of the Twelve Houses offer a further insight into the nature of the Zodiac, each House linking with a corresponding Sun sign.

The First House: ♈ Relates to the physical and mental drive and vitality of the subject. Also indicates their sub-conscious motivations, character, health and appearance.

The Second House: ♉ Concerns the material possessions and financial aspects of the subject. Governing property, resources and also the accumulation of wealth and possessions.

The Third House: ♊ Governs the immediate environment of the subject encompassing neighbours, relatives, short distance travel, communications, work and education.

The Fourth House: ♋ Concerns parents and the home. A significant indicator of a stable or broken home. Also signifies matters which are secret and hidden.

The Fifth House: ♌ Relates to the physical and mental creativity of the subject. Also leisure, pleasure, love, children, works of artistic and literary merit, gambling and speculation.

The Sixth House: ♍ Governs work and services expressed in a practical manner. Health and hygiene are stressed, indicating the physical condition of the subject and the proper functioning of their immediate environment.

The Seventh House: ♎ Outreaching and governing marital and business partnerships, the Seventh House indicates harmony or disharmony in these areas of the subject's life. Also concerns others to whom the subject wishes to relate.

The Eighth House: ♏ Rules religion and the philosophic aspect of the subject's nature. Sometimes known as 'the House of Death' which not only concerns the birth/death cycle but also wills and legacies bequeathed by others.

The Ninth House: ♐ Rules foreign travel, foreign lands and a profound degree of mental activity. Also signifies the law, the Church, realms unknown and prophecies.

The Tenth House: ♑ Encompassing the ambitions and aspirations of the subject and indicating the achievement potential. The Tenth House is known as the House of Careers and represents the father figure.

The Eleventh House: ♒ Governing the pleasures which include groups of friends or like-minded people. Concerns relationships within societies which embrace humanitarian objectives, their allied interests and aims.

The Twelfth House: ♓ Anciently called 'the House of one's own undoing', the final House governs the 'enclosed' aspect of hospitals, asylums, withdrawal and the need for privacy. It also indicates self-sacrifice and service to others.

Numerology

Numerology is the study of the symbolic and magical properties of numbers. To Pythagoras, numbers were 'the basis of all reality' – *arithmology*, a metaphysical form of arithmetic, however, is said to be the key. There are various systems upon which numerology is based, including the Hebraic version which excludes the number Nine. But, while much of the symbolism of numbers is of Kabalistic (Hebrew) origin, the comparatively simple Pythagorean system is outlined below. Numerology is a fascinating subject – by careful calculation you can assess another's character and reveal to them the significance of their own uniquely personal numbers.

The System

1	2	3	4	5	6	7	8	9
A	B	C	D	E	F	G	H	I
J	K	L	M	N	O	P	Q	R
S	T	U	V	W	X	Y	Z	

Method

Take the name you wish to 'read'. For example:

SARAH JANE JONES

Place the numerical equivalent of the vowels (Y may be used as a vowel, but only when there are no other vowels in the word) above the appropriate letters in the name. Add the numbers from left to right and encircle the final total with the Circle of Spirit. This number symbolises the inner being and subconscious motivations.

```
 1  1      1  5   6 5
SARAH JANE JONES
```

$= 19 = 1 + 9 = 10 = 1 + 0 = \textcircled{1}$

Then place the numeral equivalent of the consonants below the relevant letters. Add these numbers from left to right and place the final total in the Square of Foundation. This number indicates the outer persona and how the subject is perceived by others:

SARAH JANE JONES
1 9 8 1 5 1 5 1

= 31 = 3 + 1 = $\boxed{4}$

Add together both final totals, placing the resultant digit in a Pyramid or triangle: 1 + 4 = $\triangle{5}$

Should the two final totals add up to a double figure, say:
5 + 5 = 10, add 1 + 0 to give 1.*

This figure is the *Personality Number* and represents the subject as a whole.

Birth Number

1	2	3	4	5	6	7	8	9
Jan	Feb	Mar	Apr	May	Jun	Jul	Aug	Sep
Oct	Nov	Dec						

Sample Birth Date
January 6 1960

January is 1. Add the number(s) of the day: 6
Now add the year: 1 + 9 + 6 + 0 = 16 = 1 + 6 = 7.
Total each Birth Number calculation: 1 + 6 + 7 = 14 = 1 + 4 = 5.
Five is the *Birth Number*.

Add both the *Personality* and the *Birth* numbers together:
5 + 5 = 10 = 1 + 0 = $\star$
Place this number within a pentacle (a 5-pointed star)

You have now determined the subject's *Fate* or *Destiny Number* – the number significant to that person and the key to their future Destiny.

*In numerology, double figures are generally added together, for example, 12 = 1 + 2 = 3. However, because of their exceptionally strong individual power, the Master Numbers Eleven and Twenty-Two are the exceptions to this rule. Therefore, when you arrive at these numbers, do not reduce them further, and see the relevant interpretations.

Interpretations of Numbers 1 – 9, 11 and 22

One: The god-figure and primal generator. Ruler: The Sun. Powerful, individualistic, creative One's are forceful but obstinate. They are outgoing, courageous and willing to try out new ideas. They must not repress their vital energies. Supreme egotists, One's should balance their sense of superiority with a sense of humour.

Two: The number of polarity – male/female, positive/negative. Ruler: The Moon. Two's are givers, peacemakers, naturally reticent and tend to hypersensitivity and emotionality. Two's avoid arguments at all costs and consequently seem docile, ineffectual people. Harmony and balance are important to Two's, as are periods of quiet reflection to restore wellbeing.

Three: The Triad – body, soul, spirit. Ruler: Venus. Attractive, dynamic, extrovert and often 'stars' in their own right, Three's are charming, witty, conversant with many subjects and have considerable potential. Though with lively, productive sex lives, they often remain unattached. Three's may be arrogant and conceited, but recognition can be theirs.

Four: The number of Foundation – the four winds; the four seasons; the four astrological elements. Ruler: Saturn. Four's are stolid, 'four-square', reliable. Practical, plodding, home-loving Four's succeed through diligence and perseverance. They can be 'respectable' to a fault, defensive and stubborn, but are loyal, trustworthy 'pillars of society'.

Five: Said to be the prevailing number in Nature and Art, five symbolises Fire and the Stigmata. Ruler: Mars. Multi-talented and with many interests, Five's are attractive, independent, free-thinking, fast-moving and potentially foot-loose. Energies are often sexual. Resenting restrictions and responsibilities, Five's can be reckless and self-indulgent.

Six: Perfectly balanced and divisible by odd (3) and even (2) numbers. Ruler: Jupiter. Sixes are fair-minded, slow to anger and with Three's outgoing personality and Two's peacemaking and giving ways, are harmonious, domesticated and make excellent spouses and parents. With Four-like 'squareness', Six is stubborn, occasionally smug but always reliable.

Seven: A magical number. The sign of occultists and the esoteric. Ruler: Neptune. Seven's are secretive, mysterious, stand-offish, intuitive and introspective. An unworldly attitude means most Sevens need to be 'protected'. Life often goes in seven-year cycles. Tarot significance: 'The determination to balance hard work with times of productive solitude'.

Eight: Represents justice and balance. Ruler: The Sun. Eight's are single-minded and show good judgement and executive skills, often achieving power and material success. A capacity for hard work can result in self-made success – if so, Eight seldom lets go. Though greed and miserliness lurk within this number, it is a determined striver.

Nine: The muses number nine and, anciently, so did the planets. Ruler: All the planets. Idealistic Nine's – capable of realising those ideals – are intensely passionate people needing to control their wild impulses. Variously assertive, trusting, generous, selfish and wilful, Nine's seriously need stabilising influences. In love, they are romantic, ardent and impetuous.

Eleven: The number of genius, of saints and sinners. Ruler: Neptune. Eleven's have the potential to fulfill the heights of spiritual ambition and idealistic dreams. While disappointment can lead to dissipation and degradation, basic qualities remain undimmed.

Twenty-Two: Represents pure idealism combined with practicality. Ruler: Uranus. Twenty-two is the humanitarian, philanthropist and scientist with the gift of vision plus the intellectual means to realise that vision. Ultimately powerful because of its practicality, should the power within this number be used for evil, he or she is a formidable force!